POCKET
REFERENCE
2008

OTHER TITLES IN THE RANGE

Whitaker's Almanack

Whitaker's Concise Almanack

Whitaker's Scottish Almanack

Whitaker's Olympic Almanack

Whitaker's Almanack Quiz Book

Whitaker's Almanack Little Book of Infinity

Whitaker's Almanack Little Book of Everything

Whitaker's Almanack Little Book of Astronomy

WHITAKER'S ALMANACK

POCKET REFERENCE 2008

A & C BLACK

LONDON

A & C Black (Publishers) Ltd
38 Soho Square, London W1D 3HB
Whitaker's Almanack published annually since 1868

ISBN-10: 0-7136-8563-8
ISBN-13: 978-0-7136-8563-3

Cover images: © Alamy, Getty Images, PA Photos
Typeset by RefineCatch Ltd, Bungay, Suffolk
Printed and bound in Great Britain by William Clowes Ltd,
Beccles, Suffolk

This book is produced using paper that is made from wood grown
in managed, sustainable forests. It is natural, renewable and
recyclable. The logging and manufacturing processes conform to
the environmental regulations of the country of origin.

Whitaker's is a registered trade mark of J. Whitaker and Sons Ltd,
Registered Trade Mark Nos. (UK) 1322125/09; 13422126/16
and 1322127/41; (EU) 19960401/09, 16, 41, licensed for use
by A & C Black (Publishers) Ltd.

The publishers make no representation, express or implied, with
regard to the accuracy of the information contained in this book
and cannot accept legal responsibility for any errors or omissions
that take place.

A CIP catalogue record for this book is available from the British
Library.

Editorial Staff
Inna Ward, Clare Slaven, Mike Jakeman, Rob Hardy

CONTENTS

ETIQUETTE   **50**

FOOD AND DRINK   **60**

GEOGRAPHY   **69**

LANGUAGE 82

ROYALTY 142

SCIENCE 151

LIFE SCIENCES   **169**

SPORT   **179**

TIME 192

WEIGHTS AND MEASURES 208

FOREWORD

If you have a thirst for facts, figures and general knowledge, then *Whitaker's Almanack Pocket Reference* is just the book you need. Published annually in a conveniently sized, easy-to-use format, this edition of *Whitaker's Almanack Pocket Reference* is the essential tool for quiz and general knowledge enthusiasts, ideal for use in the home, office or classroom.

Whitaker's Almanack Pocket Reference covers a broad range of subjects answering both practical day-to-day and more esoteric queries. New in this edition are:

- Best-selling singles and albums
- A new food and drink section
- Literary aliases
- Fascinating sports stats
- Endangered species
- Fully updated countries and currencies

Political statistics, geographical and scientific data, historical lists, protocol, definitions … it's all here at your fingertips!

Whitaker's Almanack
38 Soho Square
London W1D 3HB

whitakers@acblack.com
www.whitakersalmanack.com

14

ALPHABETS AND SYMBOLS

GREEK ALPHABET

		NAME OF LETTER	TRANS-LITERATION
A	α	alpha	a
B	β	beta	b
Γ	γ	gamma	g
Δ	δ	delta	d
E	ε	epsilon	e
Z	ζ	zeta	z
H	η	eta	ē
Θ	θ	theta	th
I	ι	iota	i
K	κ	kappa	k
Λ	λ	lambda	l
M	μ	mu	m
N	ν	nu	n
Ξ	ξ	xi	x
O	ο	omicron	o
Π	π	pi	p
P	ρ	rho	r
Σ	σ	sigma	s
T	τ	tau	t
Y	υ	upsilon	u
Φ	φ	phi	ph
X	χ	chi	ch
Ψ	ψ	psi	ps
Ω	ω	omega	ō, or Ω

CYRILLIC ALPHABET

		TRANS-LITERATION
А	а	a
Б	б	b
В	в	v
Г	г	g
Д	д	d
Е	е	e, a ar ye
Ё	ё	jo or yo
Ж	ж	ž or zh
З	з	z
И	и	i
Й	й	j or ĭ
К	к	k
Л	л	l
М	м	m
Н	н	n
О	о	o
П	п	p
Р	р	r
С	с	s
Т	т	t
У	у	u
Ф	ф	f
Х	х	x or kh
Ц	ц	c or ts
Ч	ч	č or ch
Ш	ш	š or sh
Щ	щ	šč or shch
Ъ	ъ	" or "
Ы	ы	y
Ь	ь	' or '
Э	э	è or é
Ю	ю	ju or yu
Я	я	ja or ya

ANGLO-SAXON RUNIC ALPHABET

The Anglo-Saxon runic alphabet is known as the Futhorc, from the names of the first six letters.

RUNE	MODERN LETTER	NAME OF RUNE	MEANING
ᚠ	f	feoh	wealth
ᚢ	u	ur	aurochs
ᚦ	th	þorn	thorn
ᚩ	o	os	mouth
ᚱ	r	rad	riding
ᚳ	c	cen	torch
ᚷ	g	gyfu	gift
ᚹ	w	wynn	joy
ᚻ	h	hægl	hail
ᚾ	n	nyd	need
ᛁ	i	is	ice
ᛄ	j	ger	harvest
ᛇ	eo	eoh	yew
ᛈ	p	peorð	hearth
ᛉ	x	eolhxsecg	elksedge
ᛋ	s	sigel	sun
ᛏ	t	Tir	Tiw
ᛒ	b	beorc	birch
ᛖ	e	eh	horse
ᛗ	m	man	man
ᛚ	l	lagu	water
ᛝ	ng	Ing	Ing
ᛟ	oe	eþel	homeland
ᛞ	d	dæg	day
ᚪ	a	ac	oak
ᚫ	æ	æsc	ash
ᚣ	y	yr	weapon
ᛡ	ia	ior	beaver
ᛠ	ea	ear	grave

INTERNATIONAL RADIO ALPHABET

A	Alfa
B	Bravo
C	Charlie
D	Delta
E	Echo
F	Foxtrot
G	Golf
H	Hotel
I	India
J	Juliet
K	Kilo
L	Lima
M	Mike
N	November
O	Oscar
P	Papa
Q	Quebec
R	Romeo
S	Sierra
T	Tango
U	Uniform
V	Victor
W	Whisky
X	X-Ray
Y	Yankee
Z	Zulu

MORSE CODE

The International Morse Code was formulated in 1852. The spoken code enables radio operators to send messages with their own voices, using the expressions 'dah' and 'di' or 'dit' instead of keying in dashes and dots on their transmitters.

A	. —	di-dah
B	— . . .	dah-di-di-dit
C	— . — .	dah-di-dah-dit
D	— . .	dah-di-dit
E	.	dit
F	. . — .	di-di-dah-dit
G	— — .	dah-dah-dit
H	. . . .	di-di-di-dit
I	. .	di-dit
J	. — — —	di-dah-dah-dah
K	— . —	dah-di-dah
L	. — . .	di-dah-di-dit
M	— —	dah-dah
N	— .	dah-dit
O	— — —	dah-dah-dah
P	. — — .	di-dah-dah-dit
Q	— — . —	dah-dah-di-dah
R	. — .	di-dah-dit
S	. . .	di-di-dit
T	—	dah
U	. . —	di-di-dah
V	. . . —	di-di-di-dah
W	. — —	di-dah-dah
X	— . . —	dah-di-di-dah
Y	— . — —	dah-di-dah-dah
Z	— — . .	dah-dah-di-dit

Dash = dah
Dot = di or dit

BRAILLE ALPHABET AND NUMBERS

BRAILLE ALPHABET

BRAILLE NUMBERS

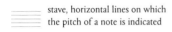

⠼⠁ 1 ⠼⠙ 4 ⠼⠛ 7 ⠼⠚ 0

⠼⠃ 2 ⠼⠑ 5 ⠼⠓ 8

⠼⠉ 3 ⠼⠋ 6 ⠼⠊ 9

MUSICAL NOTATION

stave, horizontal lines on which the pitch of a note is indicated

Clef = a sign written at the beginning of the stave to indicate the register in which the music is to be performed. There are three kinds:

 𝄞 treble, or G clef, used for the upper stave of keyboard music

 𝄢 bass, or F clef, used for the lower stave of keyboard music

 𝄡 C clef

INDICATIONS OF PITCH

 ♭ flat: lowering the note by a semi-tone

 ♯ sharp: raising the note by a semi-tone

 ♮ natural: returning a note to its original pitch

NOTE LENGTHS

SYMBOL	NAME	MEANING	REST
𝅝	semibreve	whole note	▬
𝅗𝅥	minim	half note	▬
𝅘𝅥	crotchet	quarter note	𝄽
𝅘𝅥𝅮	quaver	eighth note	𝄾
𝅘𝅥𝅯	semi-quaver	sixteenth note	𝄿

TEMPO (the term used to denote variations in speed)

TERM	MEANING
Accelerando	becoming faster
Rallentando, ritardando, ritenuto	becoming slower
Grave	very slow and solemn
Lento	slow
Largo	broadly
Adagio	in a leisurely manner
Andante	walking pace
Moderato	at a moderate speed
Allegro	lively, fairly fast
Vivace	fast
Presto	very fast
Prestissimo	as fast as possible

DYNAMICS (the term used to denote the volume of music)

SIGN	TERM	MEANING
pp	*pianissimo*	very soft
p	*piano*	soft
mp	*mezzo-piano*	moderately soft
mf	*mezzo-forte*	moderately loud
f	*forte*	loud
ff	*fortissimo*	very loud
<	*crescendo*	getting louder
>	*diminuendo*	getting softer

PERCUSSION INSTRUMENTS

Definite Pitch
Antique cymbals
Celesta
Cimbalom
Glockenspiel
Marimba
Timpani
Tubular bells
Vibraphone
Xylophone

Latin American Percussion Instruments
Bongos
Claves
Guiro
Maracas

Indefinite Pitch
Anvil
Bass drums
Castanets
Cymbals
Gong (tam-tam)
Rattle (ratchet)
Snare drum
Tabor
Temple block
Tenor drum
Tom-toms
Triangle
Whip (slapstick)
Wind machines
Wood block

WIND INSTRUMENTS

Basset horn
Bassoon
Clarinet
E flat clarinet
Flute
Flute in G
Heckelphone
Oboe
Oboe d'amore
Piccolo
Recorder
Sarrusophone
Saxophone

BRASS INSTRUMENTS

Bass Trumpet
Cornet
Flügel horn
Horn
Tenor tuba
Trombone
Trumpet
Trumpet in D
Tuba

STRING INSTRUMENTS

Cello
Double Bass
Guitar
Harp
Viola
Violin

ARRANGEMENT OF THE ORCHESTRA

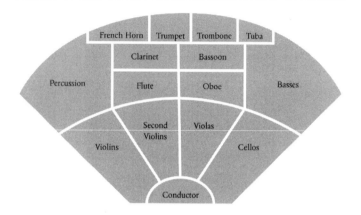

HALLMARKS

Hallmarks are the symbols stamped on gold, silver or platinum articles to indicate that they have been tested at an official Assay Office and that they conform to one of the legal standards. With certain exceptions, all gold, silver or platinum articles are required by law to be hallmarked before they are offered for sale.

Since 1 January 1999, UK hallmarks have consisted of three compulsory symbols: the sponsor's mark, the assay office mark, and the fineness (standard) mark. The date lettermark became voluntary on 1 January 1999. Additional marks have been authorised from time to time.

SPONSOR'S MARK

Instituted in England in 1363, the sponsor's mark was originally a device such as a bird or fleur-de-lis. Now it consists of the initial letters of the name or names of the manufacturer or firm. Where two or more sponsors have the same initials, there is a variation in the surrounding shield or style of letters.

FINENESS (STANDARD) MARK

The fineness (standard) mark indicates that the content of the precious metal in the alloy from which the article is made is not less than the legal standard. The legal standard is the minimum content of precious metal by weight in parts per thousand, and the standards are:

Gold	999	
	990	
	916.6	(22 carat)
	750	(18 carat)
	585	(14 carat)
	375	(9 carat)
Silver	999	
	958.4	(Britannia)
	925	(sterling)
	800	
Platinum	999	
	950	
	900	
	850	

The metals are marked as follows, if they are manufactured in the United Kingdom:

Gold – a crown followed by the millesimal figure for the standard, e.g. 916 for 22 carat

Silver – Britannia silver: a full-length figure of Britannia. Sterling silver: a lion passant (England) or a lion rampant (Scotland)

  Britannia Silver

  Sterling Silver (England)

  Sterling Silver (Scotland)

Platinum – an orb

ASSAY OFFICE MARK
This mark identifies the particular assay office at which the article was tested and marked. The British assay offices are:

 London

 Birmingham

 Sheffield

 Edinburgh

Assay offices formerly existed in other towns, e.g. Chester, Exeter, Glasgow, Newcastle, Norwich and York, each having its own distinguishing mark.

DATE LETTER
The date letter shows the year in which an article was assayed and hallmarked. Each alphabetical cycle has a distinctive style of lettering or shape of shield. The date letters were different at the various assay offices and the particular office must be established from the assay office mark before reference is made to tables of date letters.

Since 1 January 1975, each office has used the same style of date letter and shield for all articles.

OTHER MARKS
FOREIGN GOODS
Foreign goods imported into the UK are required to be hallmarked before sale, unless they already bear a convention mark (see below) or a hallmark struck by an independent assay office in the European Economic Area which is deemed to be equivalent to a UK hallmark.

The following are the assay office marks for gold imported articles. For silver and platinum the symbols remain the same but the shields differ in shape.

 London

 Birmingham

 Sheffield

 Edinburgh

CONVENTION HALLMARKS
Special marks at authorised assay offices of the signatory countries of the International Convention on Hallmarking (Austria, the Czech Republic, Denmark, Finland, Ireland, The Netherlands, Norway, Portugal, Sweden, Switzerland and the UK) are legally recognised in the United Kingdom as approved hallmarks. These consist of a sponsor's mark, a common control mark, a fineness mark (arabic numerals showing the standard in parts per thousand), and an assay office mark. There is no date letter.

The fineness marks are:

Gold	750	(18 carat)
	585	(14 carat)
	375	(9 carat)
Silver	925	(sterling)
Platinum	950	

The common control marks are:

 Gold (18 carat)

 Silver

 Platinum

HERALDRY

TERMS

Achievement: The complete pictorial display of arms comprising a shield, helmet, crest, torse, mantling and motto. Supporters, additional mottoes or rallying cries, decorations and insignia of office may also be depicted if the individual is entitled to them.

Blazon: The formula describing the design of arms of a whole achievement; or, used as a verb, to make such a description.

Escutcheon: A shield, especially a small shield placed on top of a larger to display particularly significant arms.

POINTS AND PARTS OF A SHIELD

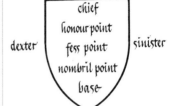

ORDINARIES

Ordinaries are simple geometric figures used in armory

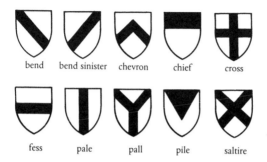

| bend | bend sinister | chevron | chief | cross |

| fess | pale | pall | pile | saltire |

DIVISIONS

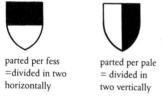

parted per fess
=divided in two
horizontally

parted per pale
= divided in
two vertically

Impaling = dividing a shield vertically and placing arms in both halves
Quartering = dividing a shield in four and placing arms in all four quarters

TINCTURES

There are five colours, three stains and two metals:

COLOURS

Gules	red
Azure	blue
Vert	green
Sable	black
Purpure	purple
Proper	an animal or object depicted in its natural colours

STAINS

Murrey	mulberry or maroon
Tenné	tawny orange
Sanguine	blood-coloured red

METALS

Or	gold; may be depicted as gilt, or painted as yellow or ochre
Argent	silver; may be painted as pale grey or be white

FURS

ermine	white field with black spots
ermines	black field with white spots
erminois	gold field with black spots
pean	black field with gold spots
vair	blue and white

ANIMALS

addorsed	two animals back to back
at gaze	looking full face
combatant	two animals face to face, in the attitude of fighting
couchant	lying, with head erect
dormant	in a sleeping posture
passant	walking, usually with right paw raised
rampant	rearing up with three paws outstretched
salient	springing up with forepaws raised
sejant	sitting
statant	standing, with all four feet down
trippant	walking, usually with right paw raised (hart, buck, stag or hind only)

Animals are usually facing to the dexter (right), but:

affronte	whole beast facing forward
guardant	face out to viewer
reguardant	looking back over shoulder

BIRDS

close	wings folded in
displayed	fully frontal, wings extended, head turned to the dexter
rising	taking flight, wings raised

Heads of birds are usually shown in profile, except for owls, which are always guardant

THE ARTS

TURNER PRIZE WINNERS

1984 Malcolm Morley
1985 Howard Hodgkin
1986 Gilbert and George
1987 Richard Deacon
1988 Tony Cragg
1989 Richard Long
1990 no prize
1991 Anish Kapoor
1992 Grenville Davey

1993 Rachel Whiteread
1994 Anthony Gormley
1995 Damien Hirst
1996 Douglas Gordon
1997 Gillian Wearing
1998 Chris Ofili
1999 Steve McQueen
2000 Wolfgang Tillmans
2001 Martin Creed
2002 Keith Tyson
2003 Grayson Perry
2004 Jeremy Deller
2005 Simon Starling
2006 Tomma Abts

BOOKER PRIZE WINNERS

1969 P. H. Newby, *Something to Answer For*
1970 Bernice Rubens, *The Elected Member*
1971 V. S. Naipaul, *In a Free State*
1972 John Berger, *G*
1973 J. G. Farrell, *The Siege of Krishnapur*
1974 Nadine Gordimer, *The Conservationist*/Stanley Middleton, *Holiday*
1975 Ruth Prawer Jhabvala, *Heat and Dust*
1976 David Storey, *Saville*
1977 Paul Scott, *Staying On*
1978 Iris Murdoch, *The Sea, The Sea*
1979 Penelope Fitzgerald, *Offshore*
1980 William Golding, *Rites of Passage*
1981 Salman Rushdie, *Midnight's Children*
1982 Thomas Keneally, *Schindler's Ark*
1983 J. M. Coetzee, *Life and Times of Michael K*
1984 Anita Brookner, *Hotel du Lac*
1985 Keri Hulme, *The Bone People*
1986 Kingsley Amis, *The Old Devils*
1987 Penelope Lively, *Moon Tiger*
1988 Peter Carey, *Oscar and Lucinda*
1989 Kazuo Ishiguro, *The Remains of the Day*
1990 A. S. Byatt, *Possession*
1991 Ben Okri, *The Famished Road*

1992 Michael Ondaatje, *The English Patient*/ Barry Unsworth, *Sacred Hunger*
1993 Roddy Doyle, *Paddy Clarke, Ha, Ha, Ha*
1994 James Kelman, *How Late It Was, How Late*
1995 Pat Barker, *The Ghost Road*
1996 Graham Swift, *Last Orders*
1997 Arundhati Roy, *The God of Small Things*
1998 Ian McEwan, *Amsterdam*
1999 J. M. Coetzee, *Disgrace*
2000 Margaret Atwood, *The Blind Assassin*
2001 Peter Carey, *True History of the Kelly Gang*
2002 Yann Martell, *The Life of Pi*
2003 D. B. C. Pierre, *Vernon God Little*
2004 Alan Hollinghurst, *The Line of Beauty*
2005 John Banville, *The Sea*
2006 Kiran Desai, *The Inheritance of Loss*

NOMS DE PLUME

Richard Bachman	*Stephen King*
Acton Bell	*Anne Brontë*
Currer Bell	*Charlotte Brontë*
Ellis Bell	*Emily Brontë*
John le Carré	*David John Moore Cornwall*
Lewis Carroll	*Charles Dodgson*
George Egerton	*Mary Chavelita Bright*
George Eliot	*Mary Ann Evans*
Nicci French	*Nicci Gerard and Sean French*
Diedrich Knickerbocker	*Washington Irving*
Molière	*Jean Baptiste Poquelin*
Toni Morrison	*Chloe Anthony Wofford*
Flann O'Brien	*Brian O'Nolan*
George Orwell	*Eric Arthur Blair*
Saki	*Hector Hugh Munro*
Lemony Snicket	*Daniel Handler*
Barbara Vine	*Ruth Rendell*
Mark Twain	*Samuel Clemens*
Mary Westmacott	*Agatha Christie*

'BEST PICTURE' OSCAR WINNERS

1928 Wings
1929 Broadway Melody
1930 All Quiet On the Western Front
1931 Cimarron
1932 Grand Hotel
1933 Cavalcade
1934 It Happened One Night
1935 Mutiny on the Bounty
1936 The Great Ziegfeld
1937 The Life of Emile Zola
1938 You Can't Take It With You
1939 Gone With the Wind
1940 Rebecca
1941 How Green Was My Valley
1942 Mrs Miniver
1943 Casablanca
1944 Going My Way
1945 The Lost Weekend
1946 The Best Years of Our Lives

1947 Gentleman's Agreement
1948 Hamlet
1949 All the King's Men
1950 All About Eve
1951 An American in Paris
1952 The Greatest Show on Earth
1953 From Here to Eternity
1954 On the Waterfront
1955 Marty
1956 Around the World in Eighty Days
1957 The Bridge on the River Kwai
1958 Gigi
1959 Ben-Hur
1960 The Apartment
1961 West Side Story
1962 Lawrence of Arabia
1963 Tom Jones
1964 My Fair Lady
1965 The Sound of Music
1966 A Man for All Seasons
1967 In the Heat of the Night
1968 Oliver!
1969 Midnight Cowboy
1970 Patton
1971 The French Connection
1972 The Godfather
1973 The Sting
1974 The Godfather Part II
1975 One Flew Over the Cuckoo's Nest
1976 Rocky
1977 Annie Hall

1978 The Deer Hunter
1979 Kramer vs Kramer
1980 Ordinary People
1981 Chariots of Fire
1982 Gandhi
1983 Terms of Endearment
1984 Amadeus
1985 Out of Africa
1986 Platoon
1987 The Last Emperor
1988 Rain Man
1989 Driving Miss Daisy
1990 Dances with Wolves
1991 The Silence of the Lambs
1992 Unforgiven
1993 Schindler's List
1994 Forrest Gump
1995 Braveheart
1996 The English Patient
1997 Titanic
1998 Shakespeare in Love
1999 American Beauty
2000 Gladiator
2001 A Beautiful Mind
2002 Chicago
2003 The Lord of the Rings:
      The Return of the King
2004 Million Dollar Baby
2005 Crash
2006 The Departed

'BEST ACTOR' OSCAR WINNERS

1928 Emil Jannings, *The Last Command*
1929 Warner Baxter, *In Old Arizona*
1930 George Arliss, *Disraeli*
1931 Lionel Barrymore, *A Free Soul*
1932 Wallace Beery, *The Champ*; Fredric March, *Dr. Jekyll and Mr. Hyde*

1933 Charles Laughton, *The Private Life of Henry VIII*
1934 Clark Gable, *It Happened One Night*†
1935 Victor McLaglen, *The Informer*
1936 Paul Muni, *The Story of Louis Pasteur*

1937 Spencer Tracy, *Captains Courageous*
1938 Spencer Tracy, *Boys Town*
1939 Robert Donat, *Goodbye Mr. Chips*
1940 James Stewart, *The Philadelphia Story*
1941 Gary Cooper, *Sergeant York*
1942 James Cagney, *Yankee Doodle Dandy*
1943 Paul Lukas, *Watch on the Rhine*
1944 Bing Crosby, *Going My Way*†
1945 Ray Milland, *The Lost Weekend*†
1946 Fredric March, *The Best Years of Our Lives*†
1947 Ronald Colman, *A Double Life*
1948 Laurence Olivier, *Hamlet*†
1949 Broderick Crawford, *All the King's Men*†
1950 José Ferrer, *Cyrano de Bergerac*
1951 Humphrey Bogart, *The African Queen*
1952 Gary Cooper, *High Noon*
1953 William Holden, *Stalag 17*
1954 Marlon Brando, *On The Waterfront*†
1955 Ernest Borgnine, *Marty*†
1956 Yul Brynner, *The King and I*
1957 Alec Guinness, *The Bridge on the River Kwai*†
1958 David Niven, *Separate Tables*
1959 Charlton Heston, *Ben-Hur*†
1960 Burt Lancaster, *Elmer Gantry*
1961 Maximilian Schell, *Judgment at Nuremberg*
1962 Gregory Peck, *To Kill a Mockingbird*
1963 Sidney Poitier, *Lilies of the Field*
1964 Rex Harrison, *My Fair Lady*†
1965 Lee Marvin, *Cat Ballou*
1966 Paul Scofield, *A Man for All Seasons*†
1967 Rod Steiger, *In the Heat of the Night*†

1968 Cliff Robertson, *Charly*
1969 John Wayne, *True Grit*
1970 George C. Scott, *Patton**†
1971 Gene Hackman, *The French Connection*†
1972 Marlon Brando, *The Godfather**†
1973 Jack Lemmon, *Save the Tiger*
1974 Art Carney, *Harry and Tonto*
1975 Jack Nicholson, *One Flew Over the Cuckoo's Nest*†
1976 Peter Finch, *Network*
1977 Richard Dreyfuss, *Jaws*
1978 Jon Voight, *Coming Home*
1979 Dustin Hoffman, *Kramer vs Kramer*†
1980 Robert De Niro, *Raging Bull*
1981 Henry Fonda, *On Golden Pond*
1982 Ben Kingsley, *Gandhi*†
1983 Robert Duvall, *Tender Mercies*
1984 F. Murray Abraham, *Amadeus*†
1985 William Hurt, *Kiss of the Spider Woman*
1986 Paul Newman, *The Color of Money*
1987 Michael Douglas, *Wall Street*
1988 Dustin Hoffman, *Rain Man*†
1989 Daniel Day-Lewis, *My Left Foot*
1990 Jeremy Irons, *Reversal of Fortune*
1991 Anthony Hopkins, *The Silence of the Lambs*†
1992 Al Pacino, *Scent of a Woman*
1993 Tom Hanks, *Philadelphia*
1994 Tom Hanks, *Forrest Gump*†
1995 Nicholas Cage, *Leaving Las Vegas*
1996 Geoffrey Rush, *Shine*
1997 Jack Nicholson, *As Good As It Gets*
1998 Roberto Benigni, *Life Is Beautiful*
1999 Kevin Spacey, *American Beauty*†
2000 Russell Crowe, *Gladiator*†
2001 Denzel Washington, *Training Day*
2002 Adrien Brody, *The Pianist*
2003 Sean Penn, *Mystic River*

2004 Jamie Foxx, *Ray*
2005 Philip Seymour Hoffman *Capote*

2006 Forest Whitaker, *The Last King of Scotland*

* indicates the actor or actress refused the award

† indicates actor or actress won their award appearing in that year's best picture

'BEST ACTRESS' OSCAR WINNERS

1928 Janet Gaynor, *Seventh Heaven*
1929 Mary Pickford, *Coquette*
1930 Norma Shearer, *The Divorcee*
1931 Marie Dressler, *Min and Bill*
1932 Helen Hayes, *The Sin of Madelon Claudet*
1933 Katharine Hepburn, *Cavalcade*
1934 Claudette Colbert, *It Happened One Night*†
1935 Bette Davis, *Of Human Bondage*
1936 Luise Rainer, *The Great Ziegfeld*†
1937 Luise Rainer, *The Good Earth*
1938 Bette Davis, *Jezebel*
1939 Vivien Leigh, *Gone with the Wind*†
1940 Ginger Rogers, *Kitty Foyle*
1941 Joan Fontaine, *Suspicion*
1942 Greer Garson, *Mrs Miniver*†
1943 Jennifer Jones, *The Song of Bernadette*
1944 Ingrid Bergman, *Gaslight*
1945 Joan Crawford, *Mildred Pierce*
1946 Olivia de Havilland, *To Each His Own*
1947 Loretta Young, *The Farmer's Daughter*
1948 Jane Wyman, *Johnny Belinda*
1949 Olivia de Havilland, *The Heiress*
1950 Judy Holliday, *Born Yesterday*
1951 Vivien Leigh, *A Streetcar Named Desire*
1952 Shirley Booth, *Come Back, Little Sheba*
1953 Audrey Hepburn, *Roman Holiday*

1954 Grace Kelly, *The Country Girl*
1955 Anna Magnani, *The Rose Tattoo*
1956 Ingrid Bergman, *Anastasia*
1957 Joanne Woodward, *The Three Faces of Eve*
1958 Susan Hayward, *I Want To Live!*
1959 Simone Signoret, *Room at the Top*
1960 Elizabeth Taylor, *Butterfield 8*
1961 Sophia Loren, *Two Women*
1962 Anne Bancroft, *The Miracle Worker*
1963 Patricia Neal, *Hud*
1964 Julie Andrews, *Mary Poppins*
1965 Julie Christie, *Darling*
1966 Elizabeth Taylor, *Who's Afraid of Virginia Woolf?*
1967 Katharine Hepburn, *Guess Who's Coming to Dinner*
1968 Katharine Hepburn, *The Lion in Winter*; Barbra Streisand, *Funny Girl*
1969 Maggie Smith, *The Prime of Miss Jean Brodie*
1970 Glenda Jackson, *Women in Love*
1971 Jane Fonda, *Klute*
1972 Liza Minnelli, *Cabaret*
1973 Glenda Jackson, *A Touch of Class*
1974 Ellen Burstyn, *Alice Doesn't Live Here Anymore*
1975 Louise Fletcher, *One Flew over the Cuckoo's Nest*†
1976 Faye Dunaway, *Network*
1977 Diane Keaton, *Annie Hall*†
1978 Jane Fonda, *Coming Home*

1979 Sally Field, *Norma Rae*	1992 Emma Thompson, *Howards End*
1980 Sissy Spacek, *Coal Miner's Daughter*	1993 Holly Hunter, *The Piano*
1981 Katharine Hepburn, *On Golden Pond*	1994 Jessica Lange, *Blue Sky*
1982 Meryl Streep, *Sophie's Choice*	1995 Susan Sarandon, *Dead Man Walking*
1983 Shirley MacLaine, *Terms of Endearment†*	1996 Frances McDormand, *Fargo*
1984 Sally Field, *Places in the Heart*	1997 Helen Hunt, *As Good As It Gets*
1985 Geraldine Page, *The Trip to Bountiful*	1998 Gwyneth Paltrow, *Shakespeare in Love†*
1986 Marlee Matlin, *Children of a Lesser God*	1999 Hilary Swank, *Boys Don't Cry*
1987 Cher, *Moonstruck*	2000 Julia Roberts, *Erin Brockovich*
1988 Jodie Foster, *The Accused*	2001 Halle Berry, *Monster's Ball*
1989 Jessica Tandy, *Driving Miss Daisy*	2002 Nicole Kidman, *The Hours*
1990 Kathy Bates, *Misery*	2003 Charlize Theron, *Monster*
1991 Jodie Foster, *The Silence of the Lambs†*	2004 Hilary Swank, *Million Dollar Baby†*
	2005 Reese Witherspoon, *Walk the Line*
	2006 Helen Mirren, *The Queen*

† indicates actor or actress won their award appearing in that year's best picture

SHAKESPEARE'S PLAYS

All's Well That Ends Well	Macbeth
Antony and Cleopatra	Measure for Measure
As You Like It	The Merchant of Venice
The Comedy of Errors	The Merry Wives of Windsor
Coriolanus	A Midsummer Night's Dream
Cymbeline	Much Ado About Nothing
Edward III	Othello
Hamlet	Pericles
Henry IV Part 1	Richard III
Henry IV Part 2	Romeo and Juliet
Henry V	The Taming of the Shrew
Henry VI Part 1	The Tempest
Henry VI Part 2	Timon of Athens
Henry VI Part 3	Titus Andronicus
Henry VIII	Troilus and Cressida
Julius Caesar	Twelfth Night
King John	The Two Gentlemen of Verona
King Lear	The Two Noble Kinsmen
Love's Labour's Lost	The Winter's Tale

PILGRIMS FROM CHAUCER'S *CANTERBURY TALES*

Knight	Physician
Miller	Pardoner
Reeve	Shipman
Cook	Prioress
Man of Law	Sir Thopas
Wife of Bath	Melibeus
Friar	Monk
Summoner	Nun's Priest
Clerk	Second Nun
Merchant	Canon's Yeoman
Squire	Manciple
Franklin	Parson

'BAD SEX AWARD' WINNERS

The Literary Review Bad Sex in Fiction Award is given annually to the author who produces the worst description of a sex scene in a novel. The award itself depicts a woman draped provocatively over an open book. It has been presented every year since 1993 and was established by literary critic Rhoda Koenig and the then editor of the *Literary Review* Auberon Waugh.

1993	Melvyn Bragg, *A Time to Dance*	2000	Sean Thomas, *Kissing England*
1994	Philip Hook, *The Stone Breakers*	2001	Christopher Hart, *Rescue Me*
1995	Philip Kerr, *Gridiron*	2002	Wedy Perriam, *Tread Softly*
1996	David Huggins, *The Big Kiss*	2003	Aniruddha Bahal, *Bunker 13*
1997	Nicholas Royle, *The Matter of the Heart*	2004	Tom Wolfe, *I am Charlotte Simmons*
1998	Sebastian Faulks, *Charlotte Gray*	2005	Giles Coren, *Winkler*
1999	A A Gill, *Starcrossed*	2006	Iain Hollingshead, *Twentysomething*

MUSICALS AND COMPOSERS

Annie Get Your Gun (1946)	Irving Berlin
Anything Goes (1934)	Cole Porter
Aspects of Love (1990)	Andrew Lloyd Webber, Don Black, Charles Hart
Carousel (1945)	Richard Rodgers and Oscar Hammerstein
Cats (1982)	Andrew Lloyd Webber
A Chorus Line (1975)	Marvin Hamlisch, Michael Bennett

Chicago (1975)	John Kander
Evita (1978)	Andrew Lloyd Webber, Tim Rice
Fiddler on the Roof (1964)	Sheldon Harnick, Jerry Bock
Godspell (1971)	Stephen Schwartz
Guys and Dolls (1950)	Frank Loesser
Hair (1967)	Galt MacDermot, James Rado, Gerome Ragni
Jesus Christ Superstar (1971)	Andrew Lloyd Webber, Tim Rice
Joseph and the Amazing Technicolour Dreamcoat (1968)	Andrew Lloyd Webber, Tim Rice
The King and I (1951)	Richard Rodgers and Oscar Hammerstein
Kiss Me Kate (1948)	Cole Porter
Les Misérables (1945)	Claude-Michel Schönberg, Alain Boublil
The Lion King (1994)	Elton John, Tim Rice
Me and My Girl (1937)	Noel Gay, Douglas Furber, Arthur Rose
Miss Saigon (1989)	Claude-Michel Schönberg, Alain Boublil
My Fair Lady (1956)	Alan J. Lerner, Frederick Loewe
Oklahoma! (1943)	Richard Rodgers and Oscar Hammerstein
Oliver! (1960)	Lionel Bart
Paint Your Wagon (1951)	Alan J. Lerner, Frederick Loewe
The Phantom of the Opera (1986)	Andrew Lloyd Webber, Charles Hart
The Sound of Music (1959)	Richard Rodgers and Oscar Hammerstein
South Pacific (1949)	Richard Rodgers and Oscar Hammerstein
Starlight Express (1984)	Andrew Lloyd Webber, Richard Stilgoe
Sunset Boulevard (1993)	Andrew Lloyd Webber, Don Black, Christopher Hampton
West Side Story (1957)	Leonard Bernstein, Stephen Sondheim

OPERAS AND COMPOSERS

Aida (1871)	Giuseppe Verdi
Ariadne auf Naxos (1912)	Richard Strauss
The Barber of Seville (1782)	Gioacchino Rossini
The Bartered Bride (1863)	Bedrich Smetana
Billy Budd (1951)	Benjamin Britten
Bluebeard's Castle (1918)	Béla Bartók
La Bohème (1896)	Giacomo Puccini
Carmen (1875)	Georges Bizet
La Cenerentola (1817)	Gioachino Rossini

Così fan tutte (1790)	Wolfgang Amadeus Mozart
The Cunning Little Vixen (1924)	Leos Janacek
Dialogues des Carmélites (1957)	Francis Poulenc
Dido and Aeneas (1689)	Henry Purcell
Don Carlo (1867)	Giuseppe Verdi
Don Giovanni (1787)	Wolfgang Amadeus Mozart
Elektra (1909)	Richard Strauss
Eugene Onegin (1879)	Pyotr Tchaikovsky
Faust (1859)	Charles Gounod
Fidelio (1805)	Ludwig van Beethoven
Die Fledermaus (1874)	Johann Strauss
The Flying Dutchman (1843)	Richard Wagner
The Gambler (1929)	Sergei Prokofiev
Götterdämmerung (1876)	Richard Wagner
Hänsel und Gretel (1893)	Engelbert Humperdinck
Jenufa (1904)	Leos Janacek
Julius Caesar (1724)	George Frideric Handel
Katya Kabanova (1921)	Leos Janacek
Lady Macbeth of Mtsensk (1934)	Dmitry Shostakovich
Madame Butterfly (1904)	Giacomo Puccini
The Magic Flute (1791)	Wolfgang Amadeus Mozart
The Marriage of Figaro (1786)	Wolfgang Amadeus Mozart
Mazeppa (1884)	Pyotr Tchaikovsky
Orfeo (1607)	Claudio Monteverdi
The Pearlfishers (1863)	Georges Bizet
Peter Grimes (1945)	Benjamin Britten
Pelléas et Mélisande (1902)	Claude Debussy
Das Rheingold (1869)	Richard Wagner
Rigoletto (1851)	Giuseppe Verdi
Rusalka (1901)	Antonin Dvorak
Salome (1905)	Richard Strauss
Tales of Hoffmann (1881)	Jacques Offenbach
Tristan and Isolde (1865)	Richard Wagner
Tosca (1900)	Giacomo Puccini
La Traviata (1853)	Giuseppe Verdi
Il Trovatore (1853)	Giuseppe Verdi
Turandot (1926)	Giacomo Puccini
War and Peace (1945)	Sergei Prokofiev
Wozzeck (1925)	Alban Berg

BEST-SELLING UK ALBUMS

	COPIES
1. Queen – *Greatest Hits* (1981)	5,400,000
2. The Beatles – *Sgt. Pepper's Lonely Hearts Club Band* (1967)	4,810,000
3. Oasis – *(What's The Story) Morning Glory?* (1995)	4,310,000
4. Dire Straits – *Brothers In Arms* (1985)	3,950,000
5. ABBA – *Gold: Greatest Hits* (1992)	3,940,000
6. Pink Floyd – *Dark Side of the Moon* (1973)	3,780,000
7. Queen – *Greatest Hits II* (1991)	3,640,000
8. Michael Jackson – *Thriller* (1982)	3,570,000
9. Michael Jackson – *Bad* (1987)	3,570,000
10. Madonna – *The Immaculate Collection* (1990)	3,400,000

Source: The Official Charts Company

BEST-SELLING UK SINGLES

	COPIES
1. Elton John – 'Candle in the Wind 1997'/'Something About the Way You Look Tonight' (1997)	4,868,000
2. Band Aid – 'Do They Know It's Christmas?' (1984)	3,550,000
3. Queen – 'Bohemian Rhapsody' (1975/1991)	2,130,000
4. Paul McCartney & Wings – 'Mull of Kintyre'/'Girls' School' (1977)	2,050,000
5. Boney M – 'Rivers of Babylon'/'Brown Girl in the Ring' (1978)	1,995,000
6. John Travolta and Olivia Newton-John – 'You're the One that I Want' (1978)	1,975,000
7. Frankie Goes To Hollywood – 'Relax' (1984)	1,191,000
8. The Beatles – 'She Loves You' (1963)	1,890,000
9. Robson Green and Jerome Flynn – 'Unchained Melody' (1995)	1,840,000
10. Boney M – 'Mary's Boy Child' (1978)	1,790,000

Source: The Official Charts Company

POETS LAUREATE

The post of Poet Laureate was officially established when John Dryden was appointed by royal warrant as Poet Laureate and Historiographer Royal in 1668, although Ben Jonson was considered to have been the first recognised laureate after having a pension of 100 marks a year conferred upon him. The post is attached to the royal household and was originally conferred on the holder for life; in 1999 the length of appointment was changed to a ten-year term. It is customary for the Poet Laureate to write verse to mark events of national importance. The postholder currently receives an honorarium of £5,000 a year.

Ben Jonson (1572–1637), appointed 1616
Sir William D'Avenant (1606–68), appointed 1638
John Dryden (1631–89), appointed 1668
Thomas Shadwell (1642–92), appointed 1689
Nahum Tate (1652–1715), appointed 1692
Nicholas Rowe (1674–1718), appointed 1715
Laurence Eusden (1688–1730), appointed 1718
Colley Cibber (1671–1757), appointed 1730
William Whitehead (1715–85), appointed 1757
Thomas Warton (1728–90), appointed 1785
Henry Pye (1745–1813), appointed 1790
Robert Southey (1774–1843), appointed 1813
William Wordsworth (1770–1850), appointed 1843
Alfred, Lord Tennyson (1809–92), appointed 1850
Alfred Austin (1835–1913), appointed 1896
Robert Bridges (1844–1930), appointed 1913
John Masefield (1878–1967), appointed 1930
Cecil Day Lewis (1904–72), appointed 1968
Sir John Betjeman (1906–84), appointed 1972
Ted Hughes (1930–98), appointed 1984
Andrew Motion (1952–), appointed 1999

BRITISH POLITICS

GENERAL ELECTIONS SINCE 1900

YEAR	DATE	PARTY FORMING THE GOVERNMENT
1900	28 Sept–24 Oct	Conservative
1906	12 Jan–7 Feb	Liberal
1910	14 Jan–9 Feb	Liberal
1910	2–19 Dec	Liberal
1918	14 Dec	Coalition*
1922	15 Nov	Conservative
1923	6 Dec	Coalition†
1924	29 Oct	Conservative
1929	30 May	Labour
1931	27 Oct	National Government‡
1935	14 Nov	Conservative
1945	5 July	Labour
1950	23 Feb	Labour
1951	25 Oct	Conservative
1955	26 May	Conservative
1959	8 Oct	Conservative
1964	15 Oct	Labour
1966	31 March	Labour
1970	18 June	Conservative
1974	28 Feb	Labour
1974	10 Oct	Labour
1979	3 May	Conservative
1983	9 June	Conservative
1987	11 June	Conservative
1992	9 April	Conservative
1997	1 May	Labour
2001	7 June	Labour
2005	5 May	Labour

* Coalition of Coalition Unionist (335 seats), Coalition Liberal (133) and Coalition Labour (10); opposition parties 229 seats, including 28 Liberal and 63 Labour

† Coalition of Labour (191 seats) and Liberal (159); opposition parties 265 seats, including Conservative 258

‡ National Government of Conservative (473 seats), Liberal National (35), Liberal (33) and National Labour (13); opposition parties 61 seats, including Labour 52 and Independent Liberal 4

PRIME MINISTERS

The accession of George I, who was unfamiliar with the English language, led to a disinclination on the part of the Sovereign to preside at meetings of his Ministers and caused the appearance of a Prime Minister, a position first acquired by Robert Walpole in 1721 and retained by him without interruption for 20 years and 326 days. The office of Prime Minister was officially recognised in 1905.

The Prime Minister, by tradition also First Lord of the Treasury and Minister for the Civil Service, is appointed by the Sovereign and is usually the leader of the party which enjoys, or can secure, a majority in the House of Commons. Other ministers are appointed by the Sovereign on the recommendation of the Prime Minister, who also allocates functions amongst ministers and has the power to obtain their resignation or dismissal individually.

Over the centuries there has been some variation in the determination of the dates of appointment of Prime Ministers. Where possible, the date given is that on which a new Prime Minister kissed the Sovereign's hands and accepted the commission to form a ministry. However, until the middle of the 19th century the dating of a commission or transfer of seals could be the date of taking office. Where the composition of the government changed, e.g. became a coalition, but the Prime Minister remained the same, the date of the change of government is given.

YEAR APPOINTED

1721	Sir Robert Walpole	*Whig*
1742	The Earl of Wilmington	*Whig*
1743	Henry Pelham	*Whig*
1754	The Duke of Newcastle	*Whig*
1756	The Duke of Devonshire	*Whig*
1757	The Duke of Newcastle	*Whig*
1762	The Earl of Bute	*Tory*
1763	George Grenville	*Whig*
1765	The Marquess of Rockingham	*Whig*
1766	The Earl of Chatham	*Whig*
1767	The Duke of Grafton	*Whig*
1770	Lord North	*Tory*
1782 *March*	The Marquess of Rockingham	*Whig*
1782 *July*	The Earl of Shelburne	*Whig*
1783 *April*	The Duke of Portland	*Coalition*
1783 *Dec.*	William Pitt	*Tory*
1801	Henry Addington	*Tory*
1804	William Pitt	*Tory*
1806	The Lord Grenville	*Whig*
1807	The Duke of Portland	*Tory*

YEAR APPOINTED		
1809	Spencer Perceval	*Tory*
1812	The Earl of Liverpool	*Tory*
1827 *April*	George Canning	*Tory*
1827 *Aug.*	Viscount Goderich	*Tory*
1828	The Duke of Wellington	*Tory*
1830	The Earl Grey	*Whig*
1834 *July*	The Viscount Melbourne	*Whig*
1834 *Nov.*	The Duke of Wellington	*Tory*
1834 *Dec.*	Sir Robert Peel	*Tory*
1835	The Viscount Melbourne	*Whig*
1841	Sir Robert Peel	*Tory*
1846	Lord John Russell (later The Earl Russell)	*Whig*
1852 *Feb.*	The Earl of Derby	*Tory*
1852 *Dec.*	The Earl of Aberdeen	*Peelite*
1855	The Viscount Palmerston	*Liberal*
1858	The Earl of Derby	*Conservative*
1859	The Viscount Palmerston	*Liberal*
1865	The Earl Russell	*Liberal*
1866	The Earl of Derby	*Conservative*
1868 *Feb.*	Benjamin Disraeli	*Conservative*
1868 *Dec.*	William Gladstone	*Liberal*
1874	Benjamin Disraeli	*Conservative*
1880	William Gladstone	*Liberal*
1885	The Marquess of Salisbury	*Conservative*
1886 *Feb.*	William Gladstone	*Liberal*
1886 *July*	The Marquess of Salisbury	*Conservative*
1892	William Gladstone	*Liberal*
1894	The Earl of Rosebery	*Liberal*
1895	The Marquess of Salisbury	*Conservative*
1902	Arthur Balfour	*Conservative*
1905	Sir Henry Campbell-Bannerman	*Liberal*
1908	Herbert Asquith	*Liberal*
1915	Herbert Asquith	*Coalition*
1916	David Lloyd-George	*Coalition*
1922	Andrew Bonar Law	*Conservative*
1923	Stanley Baldwin	*Conservative*
1924 *Jan.*	Ramsay MacDonald	*Labour*
1924 *Nov.*	Stanley Baldwin	*Conservative*
1929	Ramsay MacDonald	*Labour*
1931	Ramsay MacDonald	*Coalition*

YEAR APPOINTED

1935	Stanley Baldwin	*Coalition*
1937	Neville Chamberlain	*Coalition*
1940	Winston Churchill	*Coalition*
1945 *May*	Winston Churchill	*Conservative*
1945 *July*	Clement Attlee	*Labour*
1951	Sir Winston Churchill	*Conservative*
1955	Sir Anthony Eden	*Conservative*
1957	Harold Macmillan	*Conservative*
1963	Sir Alec Douglas-Home	*Conservative*
1964	Harold Wilson	*Labour*
1970	Edward Heath	*Conservative*
1974	Harold Wilson	*Labour*
1976	James Callaghan	*Labour*
1979	Margaret Thatcher	*Conservative*
1990	John Major	*Conservative*
1997	Tony Blair	*Labour*
2007	Gordon Brown	*Labour*

LEADERS OF THE OPPOSITION

The office of Leader of the Opposition was officially recognised in 1937 and a salary was assigned to the post.

YEAR APPOINTED

1916	Herbert Asquith	*Liberal*
1918	William Adamson	*Labour*
1921	John Clynes	*Labour*
1922	Ramsay MacDonald (leader of official Opposition)	*Labour*
1924	Stanley Baldwin	*Conservative*
1929	Stanley Baldwin	*Conservative*
1931	Arthur Henderson (leader of Labour Opposition)	*Labour*
1931	George Lansbury	*Labour*
1935	Clement Attlee	*Labour*
1945	Clement Attlee	*Labour*
1945	Winston Churchill	*Conservative*
1951	Clement Attlee	*Labour*
1955	Hugh Gaitskell	*Labour*
1963	Harold Wilson	*Labour*
1965	Edward Heath	*Conservative*
1974	Edward Heath	*Conservative*
1970	Harold Wilson	*Labour*
1975	Margaret Thatcher	*Conservative*
1979	James Callaghan	*Labour*
1980	Michael Foot	*Labour*
1983	Neil Kinnock	*Labour*
1992	John Smith	*Labour*
1994	Tony Blair	*Labour*
1997	William Hague	*Conservative*
2001	Iain Duncan Smith	*Conservative*
2003	Michael Howard	*Conservative*
2005	David Cameron	*Conservative*

SPEAKERS OF THE COMMONS SINCE 1660

The Speaker of the House of Commons is the spokesman and president of the Chamber. He or she is elected by the House at the beginning of each Parliament or when the previous Speaker retires or dies. The Speaker neither speaks in debates nor votes in divisions except when the voting is equal.

The appointment requires royal approbation before it is confirmed. The present Speaker is the 156th.

PARLIAMENT OF ENGLAND

YEAR APPOINTED

1660	Sir Harbottle Grimston
1661	Sir Edward Turner
1673	Sir Job Charlton
1678 *Feb.*	Sir Edward Seymour
1678 *April*	Sir Robert Sawyer
1679	Sir William Gregory
1680	Sir William Williams
1685	Sir John Trevor
1689	Henry Powle
1690	Sir John Trevor
1695	Paul Foley
1698	Sir Thomas Lyttleton
1701	Robert Harley (Earl of Oxford and Mortimer)
1705	John Smith

PARLIAMENT OF GREAT BRITAIN

1708	Sir Richard Onslow (Lord Onslow)
1710	William Bromley
1714	Sir Thomas Hanmer
1715	Spencer Compton (Earl of Wilmington)
1728	Arthur Onslow
1761	Sir John Cust
1770	Sir Fletcher Norton (Lord Grantley)
1780	Charles Cornwall
1789 *Jan.*	Hon. William Grenville (Lord Grenville)
1789 *June*	Henry Addington (Viscount Sidmouth)

PARLIAMENT OF UNITED KINGDOM

1801	Sir John Mitford (Lord Redesdale)
1802	Charles Abbot (Lord Colchester)
1817	Charles Manners-Sutton (Viscount Canterbury)
1835	James Abercromby (Lord Dunfermline)
1839	Charles Shaw-Lefevre (Viscount Eversley)
1857	J. Evelyn Denison (Viscount Ossington)
1872	Sir Henry Brand (Viscount Hampden)
1884	Arthur Wellesley Peel (Viscount Peel)
1895	William Gully (Viscount Selby)
1905	James Lowther (Viscount Ullswater)
1921	John Whitley
1928	Hon. Edward Fitzroy
1943	Douglas Clifton-Brown (Viscount Ruffside)
1951	William Morrison (Viscount Dunrossil)
1959	Sir Harry Hylton-Foster
1965	Horace King (Lord Maybray-King)
1971	Selwyn Lloyd (Lord Selwyn-Lloyd)
1976	George Thomas (Viscount Tonypandy)
1983	Bernard Weatherill (Lord Weatherill)
1992	Betty Boothroyd (Baroness Boothroyd of Sandwell)
2000	Michael Martin

CHANCELLORS OF THE EXCHEQUER SINCE 1900

YEAR APPOINTED		YEAR APPOINTED	
1895	Sir Michael Hicks-Beach	1931	Neville Chamberlain
1902	Charles Ritchie	1937	Sir John Simon
1903	Austen Chamberlain	1940	Sir Kingsley Wood
1905	Herbert Asquith	1943	Sir John Anderson
1908	David Lloyd George	1945	Hugh Dalton
1915	Reginald McKenna	1947	Sir Stafford Cripps
1916	Andrew Bonar Law	1950	Hugh Gaitskell
1919	Austen Chamberlain	1951	R. A. Butler
1921	Sir Robert Horne	1955	Harold Macmillan
1922	Stanley Baldwin	1957	Peter Thorneycroft
1923	Neville Chamberlain	1958	Derick Heathcoat Amory
1924 *Jan.*	Philip Snowden	1960	Selwyn Lloyd
1924 *Nov.*	Winston Churchill	1962	Reginald Maudling
1929	Philip Snowden	1964	James Callaghan

YEAR APPOINTED		YEAR APPOINTED	
1967	Roy Jenkins	1989	John Major
1970 *June*	Iain Macleod	1990	Norman Lamont
1970 *July*	Anthony Barber	1993	Kenneth Clarke
1974	Denis Healey	1997	Gordon Brown
1979	Sir Geoffrey Howe	2007	Alistair Darling
1983	Nigel Lawson		

FOREIGN SECRETARIES SINCE 1900

In 1782 the Northern Department was converted into the Foreign Office, and Charles James Fox was appointed first Secretary of State for Foreign Affairs. With the merger of the Foreign Office and the Commonwealth Office on 1 October 1968 the post was redesignated as Secretary of State for Foreign and Commonwealth Affairs.

YEAR APPOINTED		YEAR APPOINTED	
1895	Marquess of Salisbury	1963	R. A. Butler
1900	Marquess of Lansdowne	1964	Patrick Gordon Walker
1905	Sir Edward Grey	1965	Michael Stewart
1916	Arthur Balfour	1966	George Brown
1919	Earl Curzon	1968	Michael Stewart
1924 *Jan.*	Ramsay MacDonald	1970	Sir Alec Douglas-Home
1924 *Nov.*	Sir Austen Chamberlain	1974	James Callaghan
1929	Arthur Henderson	1976	Anthony Crosland
1931 *Aug.*	Marquess of Reading	1977	David Owen
1931 *Nov.*	Sir John Simon	1979	Lord Carrington
1935 *June*	Sir Samuel Hoare	1982	Francis Pym
1935 *Dec.*	Anthony Eden	1983	Sir Geoffrey Howe
1938	Viscount Halifax	1989 *July*	John Major
1940	Anthony Eden	1989 *Nov.*	Douglas Hurd
1945	Ernest Bevin	1995	Malcolm Rifkind
1951 *March*	Herbert Morrison	1997	Robin Cook
1951 *Oct.*	Anthony Eden	2001	Jack Straw
1955 *April*	Harold Macmillan	2006	Margaret Beckett
1955 *Dec.*	Selwyn Lloyd	2007	David Miliband
1960	Earl of Home		

HOME SECRETARIES SINCE 1900

In 1782 the Southern Department was converted into the Home Office. The conduct of war was removed from the Home Secretary's hands in 1794 to a separate Secretary for War. Colonies were similarly transferred in 1801 to the Secretary for War and Colonies.

YEAR APPOINTED	
1895	Sir Matthew White-Ridley
1900	Charles Ritchie
1902	Aretas Akers-Douglas
1905	Herbert Gladstone
1910	Winston Churchill
1911	Reginald McKenna
1915	Sir John Simon
1916 *Jan.*	Herbert Samuel
1916 *Dec.*	Sir George Cave
1919	Edward Shortt
1922	William Bridgeman
1924 *Jan.*	Arthur Henderson
1924 *Nov.*	Sir William Joynson-Hicks
1929	John Clynes
1931	Sir Herbert Samuel
1932	Sir John Gilmour
1935	Sir John Simon
1937	Sir Samuel Hoare
1939	Sir John Anderson
1940	Herbert Morrison
1945 *May*	Sir Donald Somervell
1945 *Aug.*	Chuter Ede
1951	Sir David Maxwell-Fyfe

YEAR APPOINTED	
1954	Gwilym Lloyd-George
1957	R. A. Butler
1962	Henry Brooke
1964	Sir Frank Soskice
1965	Roy Jenkins
1967	James Callaghan
1970	Reginald Maudling
1972	Robert Carr
1974	Roy Jenkins
1976	Merlyn Rees
1979	William Whitelaw
1983	Leon Brittan
1985	Douglas Hurd
1989	David Waddington
1990	Kenneth Baker
1992	Kenneth Clarke
1993	Michael Howard
1997	Jack Straw
2001	David Blunkett
2004	Charles Clarke
2006	John Reid
2007	Jacqui Smith

LORD CHANCELLORS SINCE 1900

YEAR APPOINTED		YEAR APPOINTED	
1895	Lord Halsbury	1945	Lord Jowitt
1905	Lord Loreburn	1951	Lord Simonds
1912	Lord Haldane	1954	Viscount Kilmuir
1915	Lord Buckmaster	1962	Lord Dilhorne
1916	Lord Finlay	1964	Lord Gardiner
1919	Lord Birkenhead	1970	Lord Hailsham of St Marylebone
1922	Viscount Cave		
1924 *Jan.*	Viscount Haldane	1974	Lord Elwyn-Jones
1924 *Nov.*	Viscount Cave	1979	Lord Hailsham of St Marylebone
1928	Lord Hailsham		
1929	Lord Sankey	1987 *June*	Lord Havers
1935	Viscount Hailsham	1987 *Oct.*	Lord Mackay of Clashfern
1938	Lord Maugham	1997	Lord Irvine of Lairg
1939	Viscount Caldecote	2003	Lord Falconer of Thoroton
1940	Viscount Simon	2007	Jack Straw

The Lord Chancellor's role was significantly altered by the Constitutional Reform Act 2005. The office holder is no longer Speaker of the House of Lords or head of the judiciary in England and Wales, and is instead a cabinet minister (the Secretary of State for Justice).

POLITICAL PARTIES AND LEADERS SINCE 1900

CONSERVATIVE PARTY

In the early 19th century the Tory Party became known as 'Conservative', to indicate that the preservation of national institutions was the leading principle of the party.

Until 1922, when the Conservatives were in opposition there were separate leaders of the Conservative Party in the House of Commons and the House of Lords. In the following list, the leaders in the Commons for the relevant years are given (*).

LEADERS OF THE CONSERVATIVE PARTY

1900	Marquess of Salisbury
1902	Arthur Balfour
1911	Andrew Bonar Law*
1921	Austen Chamberlain*
1922	Andrew Bonar Law*
1923	Stanley Baldwin
1937	Neville Chamberlain
1940	Winston Churchill
1955	Sir Anthony Eden
1957	Harold Macmillan
1963	Sir Alec Douglas-Home
1965	Edward Heath
1975	Margaret Thatcher
1990	John Major
1997	William Hague
2001	Iain Duncan Smith
2003	Michael Howard
2005	David Cameron

LABOUR PARTY

Labour candidates first stood for Parliament at the general election of 1892, when there were 27 standing as Labour or Liberal-Labour. In 1900 the Labour Representation Committee (LRC) was set up in order to establish a distinct Labour group in parliament. In 1906 the LRC became known as the Labour Party. From 1922 to 1981, when in opposition, the Parliamentary Labour Party elected its leader at the beginning of each session; most elections were uncontested.

CHAIRMEN OF THE PARLIAMENTARY LABOUR PARTY

1906	Keir Hardie
1908	Arthur Henderson
1910	George Barnes
1911	Ramsay MacDonald
1914	Arthur Henderson
1917	William Adamson

CHAIRMEN AND LEADERS OF THE PARLIAMENTARY LABOUR PARTY

1922	Ramsay MacDonald
1931	Arthur Henderson*
1932	George Lansbury
1935	Clement Attlee
1955	Hugh Gaitskell
1963	Harold Wilson

LEADERS OF THE PARLIAMENTARY LABOUR PARTY

1970	Harold Wilson
1976	James Callaghan

LEADERS OF THE LABOUR PARTY

1978	James Callaghan
1980	Michael Foot
1983	Neil Kinnock
1992	John Smith
1994	Tony Blair
2007	Gordon Brown

*Arthur Henderson lost his seat in the 1931 election. The acting leader of the Parliamentary Labour Party in 1931 was George Lansbury

LIBERAL DEMOCRAT PARTY

In 1828 the Whigs became known as 'Liberals', a name gradually accepted by the party to indicate its claim to be champions of political reform and progressive legislation.

The Liberal Party split in 1916 into two factions, which merged again following the 1922 election. In 1931 the party split into three factions: the Liberals, led by Sir Herbert Samuel; the Independent Liberals, led by David Lloyd George; and the National Liberals, led by Sir John Simon. The Independent Liberals rejoined the Liberals in the mid-1930s; the National Liberals gradually merged with the Conservative Party. After 1981 the Liberal Party formed an alliance with the Social Democratic Party (SDP), and in 1988 a majority of the Liberals agreed on a merger with the SDP under the title Social and Liberal

Democrats; since 1989 they have been known as the Liberal Democrats.

A minority continue separately as the Liberal Party.

LEADERS OF THE LIBERAL PARTY

1900	Sir Henry Campbell-Bannerman
1908	Herbert Asquith
1926	David Lloyd George
1931	Sir Herbert Samuel
1935	Sir Archibald Sinclair
1945	Clement Davies
1956	Jo Grimond
1967	Jeremy Thorpe
1976	David Steel

LEADERS OF THE LIBERAL DEMOCRATS

1988	David Steel*/Robert Maclennan*
1988	Paddy Ashdown
1999	Charles Kennedy
2006	Menzies Campbell

*David Steel and Robert Maclennan merged their respective parties into the Liberal Democrats and were joint leaders until a new leader was elected

SOCIAL DEMOCRATIC PARTY

The Council for Social Democracy was announced by four former Labour Cabinet Ministers in January 1981 and on 26 March 1981 the Social Democratic Party (SDP) was launched. Later that year the SDP and the Liberal Party formed an electoral alliance. In 1988 a majority of the SDP agreed on a merger with the Liberal Party (see above) but a minority continued as a separate party under the SDP title.

In 1990 it was decided to wind up the party organisation and its three sitting MPs became independent social democrats.

LEADERS OF THE SDP

1982	Roy Jenkins
1983	David Owen
1987	Robert Maclennan
1988	David Owen

ETIQUETTE

FORMS OF ADDRESS

This list covers the forms of address for peers, baronets and knights, their wives and children, and Privy Counsellors.

Both formal and social forms of address are given where usage differs; nowadays, the social form is generally preferred to the formal, which increasingly is used only for official documents and on very formal occasions.

F— represents forename

S— represents surname

BARON
Envelope (formal), The Right Hon. Lord—; (social), The Lord—.
Letter (formal), My Lord; (social), Dear Lord—.
Spoken, Lord—.

BARON'S WIFE
Envelope (formal), The Right Hon. Lady—; (social), The Lady—.
Letter (formal), My Lady; (social), Dear Lady—.
Spoken, Lady—.

BARON'S CHILDREN
Envelope, The Hon. F— S—.
Letter, Dear Mr/Miss/Mrs S—.
Spoken, Mr/Miss/Mrs S—.

BARONESS IN OWN RIGHT
Envelope, may be addressed in same way as a Baron's wife or, if she prefers (formal),
The Right Hon. the Baroness—; (social), The Baroness—.
Otherwise as for a Baron's wife.

BARONET
Envelope, Sir F— S—, Bt.
Letter (formal), Dear Sir; (social), Dear Sir F—.
Spoken, Sir F—.

BARONET'S WIFE
Envelope, Lady S—.
Letter (formal), Dear Madam; (social), Dear Lady S—.
Spoken, Lady S—.

COUNTESS IN OWN RIGHT
As for an Earl's wife.

COURTESY TITLES
The heir apparent to a Duke, Marquess or Earl uses the highest of his father's other titles as a courtesy title. The holder of a courtesy title is not styled The Most Hon. or The Right Hon., and in correspondence 'The' is omitted before the title. The heir apparent to a Scottish title may use the title 'Master' (see below).

DAME
Envelope, Dame F— S—, followed by appropriate postnominal letters.
Letter (formal), Dear Madam; (social), Dear Dame F—.
Spoken, Dame F—.

DUKE
Envelope (formal), His Grace the Duke of—; (social), The Duke of—.
Letter (formal), My Lord Duke; (social), Dear Duke.
Spoken (formal), Your Grace; (social), Duke.

DUKE'S WIFE
Envelope (formal), Her Grace the Duchess of—; (social), The Duchess of—.
Letter (formal), Dear Madam; (social), Dear Duchess.
Spoken, Duchess.

DUKE'S ELDEST SON
See Courtesy titles.

DUKE'S YOUNGER SONS
Envelope, Lord F— S—.
Letter (formal), My Lord; (social), Dear Lord F—.
Spoken (formal), My Lord; (social), Lord F—.

DUKE'S DAUGHTER
Envelope, Lady F— S—.
Letter (formal), Dear Madam; (social), Dear Lady F—.
Spoken, Lady F—.

EARL
Envelope (formal), The Right Hon. the Earl (of)—; (social), The Earl (of)—.
Letter (formal), My Lord; (social), Dear Lord—.
Spoken (formal), My Lord; (social), Lord—.

EARL'S WIFE
Envelope (formal), The Right Hon. the Countess (of)—; (social), The Countess (of) —.
Letter (formal), Madam; (social), Lady—.
Spoken (formal), Madam; (social), Lady—.

EARL'S CHILDREN
Eldest son, see Courtesy titles.
Younger sons, The Hon. F— S— (for forms of address, see Baron's children).
Daughters, Lady F— S— (for forms of address, see Duke's daughter).

KNIGHT (BACHELOR)
Envelope, Sir F— S—.
Letter (formal), Dear Sir; (social), Dear Sir F—.
Spoken, Sir F—.

KNIGHT (ORDERS OF CHIVALRY)
Envelope, Sir F— S—, followed by appropriate postnominal letters.
Otherwise as for Knight Bachelor.

KNIGHT'S WIFE
As for Baronet's wife.

LIFE PEER
As for Baron or for Baroness in own right.

LIFE PEER'S WIFE
As for Baron's wife.

LIFE PEER'S CHILDREN
As for Baron's children.

MARQUESS
Envelope (formal), The Most Hon. the Marquess of—; (social), The Marquess of—.
Letter (formal), My Lord; (social), Dear Lord—.
Spoken (formal), My Lord; (social), Lord—.

MARQUESS'S WIFE
Envelope (formal), The Most Hon. the Marchioness of—; (social),
The Marchioness of—.
Letter (formal), Madam; (social), Dear Lady—.
Spoken, Lady—.

MARQUESS'S CHILDREN
Eldest son, see Courtesy titles.
Younger sons, Lord F— S— (for forms of address, see Duke's younger sons).
Daughters, Lady F— S— (for forms of address, see Duke's daughter).

MASTER
The title is used by the heir apparent to a Scottish peerage, though usually the heir
apparent to a Duke, Marquess or Earl uses his courtesy title rather than 'Master'.

Envelope, The Master of—.
Letter (formal), Dear Sir; (social), Dear Master of—.
Spoken (formal), Master, or Sir; (social), Master, or Mr S—.

MASTER'S WIFE
Addressed as for the wife of the appropriate peerage style, otherwise as Mrs S—.

PRIVY COUNSELLOR
Envelope, The Right (or Rt.) Hon. F— S—.
Letter, Dear Mr/Miss/Mrs S—.
Spoken, Mr/Miss/Mrs S—.

It is incorrect to use the letters PC after the name in conjunction with the prefix
The Right Hon., unless the Privy Counsellor is a peer below the rank of Marquess
and so is styled The Right Hon. because of his rank. In this case only, the postnominal letters may be used in conjunction with the prefix The Right Hon.

VISCOUNT
Envelope (formal), The Right Hon. the Viscount—; (social), The Viscount—.
Letter (formal), My Lord; (social), Dear Lord—.
Spoken, Lord—.

VISCOUNT'S WIFE
Envelope (formal), The Right Hon. the Viscountess—; (social), The Viscountess—.
Letter (formal), Madam; (social), Dear Lady—.
Spoken, Lady—.

VISCOUNT'S CHILDREN
As for Baron's children.

ORDER OF POSTNOMINAL INITIALS

Postnominal initials appear in the following order:
1   Orders and decorations conferred by the Crown (see below)
2   Appointments to the Queen, e.g. PC, ADC
3   University degrees
4   Religious orders, e.g. OSB, SJ
5   Medical qualifications
6   Fellowships of learned societies
7   Royal academies of art
8   Fellowships of professional institutions, associations
9   Writers to the Signet (WS)
10   Appointments
11   Memberships of the armed forces

ORDERS AND DECORATIONS
Bt.   (Baronet) precedes all other letters after the surname
Kt.   (Knight Bachelor) (postnominal initials not usually used)
VC   Victoria Cross
GC   George Cross

ORDERS OF CHIVALRY, ETC.

Initials in parenthesis are of honours no longer awarded, though holders of these honours may still be alive.

KG	Knight/Lady Companion of the Order of the Garter
KT	Knight of the Order of the Thistle
(KP)	Knight of the Order of St Patrick
GCB	Knight/Dame Grand Cross of the Order of the Bath
OM	Order of Merit
(GCSI)	Knight Grand Commander of the Order of the Star of India
GCMG	Knight/Dame Grand Cross of the Order of St Michael and St George
(GCIE)	Knight Grand Commander of the Order of the Indian Empire
(CI)	Order of the Crown of India
GCVO	Knight/Dame Grand Cross of the Royal Victorian Order
GBE	Knight/Dame Grand Cross of the Order of the British Empire
CH	Companion of Honour
KCB/DCB	Knight/Dame Commander of the Order of the Bath
(KCSI)	Knight Commander of the Order of the Star of India
KCMG/ DCMG	Knight/Dame Commander of the Order of St Michael and St George
(KCIE)	Knight Commander of the Order of the Indian Empire
KCVO/ DCVO	Knight/Dame Commander of the Royal Victorian Order
KBE/DBE	Knight/Dame Commander of the Order of the British Empire
CB	Companion of the Order of the Bath
(CSI)	Companion of the Order of the Star of India
CMG	Companion of the Order of St Michael and St George
(CIE)	Companion of the Order of the Indian Empire
CVO	Commander of the Royal Victorian Order
CBE	Commander of the Order of the British Empire
DSO	Distinguished Service Order
LVO	Lieutenant of the Royal Victorian Order
OBE	Officer of the Order of the British Empire
(ISO)	Imperial Service Order
MVO	Member of the Royal Victorian Order
MBE	Member of the Order of the British Empire

DECORATIONS

CGC	Conspicuous Gallantry Cross
DSC	Distinguished Service Cross
MC	Military Cross
DFC	Distinguished Flying Cross
AFC	Air Force Cross

OTHER MEDALS*

DCM	Distinguished Conduct Medal
CGM	Conspicuous Gallantry Medal
GM	George Medal
QPM	Queen's Police Medal for gallantry
DSM	Distinguished Service Medal
MM	Military Medal
DFM	Distinguished Flying Medal
AFM	Air Force Medal
CPM	Colonial Police Medal for gallantry
RVM	Royal Victorian Medal
BEM	British Empire Medal
QPM	Queen's Police Medal for distinguished service
QFSM	Queen's Fire Service Medal for distinguished service

EFFICIENCY AND LONG SERVICE DECORATIONS, ETC.*

ERD	Army Emergency Reserve Decoration
(VD)	Volunteer Officers' Decoration
TD	Territorial Decoration
ED	Efficiency Decoration
RD	Decoration for Officers of the Royal Naval Reserve
(VRD)	Decoration for Officers of the Royal Naval Volunteer Reserve
AE	Air Efficiency Award

APPOINTMENTS

In the following order:

QC	Queen's Counsel (until appointed to the High Court)
MP	Member of Parliament
JP	Justice of the Peace
DL	Deputy Lord Lieutenant

*These lists are not all-inclusive but contain the most commonly awarded medals, decorations and qualifications

RANKS IN THE ARMED FORCES

(The numbers indicate equivalent ranks in each service)

ROYAL NAVY

1   Admiral of the Fleet
2   Admiral (Adm.)
3   Vice-Admiral (Vice-Adm.)
4   Rear-Admiral (Rear-Adm.)
5   Commodore (Cdre)
6   Captain (Capt.)
7   Commander (Cdr)
8   Lieutenant-Commander (Lt.-Cdr)
9   Lieutenant (Lt.)
10   Sub-Lieutenant (Sub-Lt.)
11   Acting Sub-Lieutenant (Acting Sub-Lt.)

ARMY

1   Field Marshal
2   General (Gen.)
3   Lieutenant-General (Lt.-Gen.)
4   Major-General (Maj.-Gen.)
5   Brigadier (Brig.)
6   Colonel (Col.)
7   Lieutenant-Colonel (Lt.-Col.)
8   Major (Maj.)
9   Captain (Capt.)
10   Lieutenant (Lt.)
11   Second Lieutenant (2nd Lt.)

ROYAL AIR FORCE

1   Marshal of the RAF
2   Air Chief Marshal
3   Air Marshal
4   Air Vice-Marshal
5   Air Commodore (Air Cdre)
6   Group Captain (Gp Capt.)
7   Wing Commander (Wg Cdr)
8   Squadron Leader (Sqn. Ldr.)
9   Flight Lieutenant (Flt. Lt)
10   Flying Officer (FO)
11   Pilot Officer (PO)

FLAG-FLYING DAYS on government buildings

The correct orientation of the Union Flag when flying is with the broader diagonal band of white uppermost in the hoist (i.e. near the pole) and the narrower diagonal band of white uppermost in the fly (i.e. furthest from the pole).

It is the practice to fly the Union Flag daily on some customs houses. In all other cases, flags are flown on government buildings by command of the Queen. The flying of the Union Flag is decided by the Department for Culture, Media and Sport at the Queen's command. On the days appointed, the Union Flag is flown on government buildings in the United Kingdom from 8am to sunset.

20 January	Birthday of the Countess of Wessex
6 February	The Queen's Accession
19 February	Birthday of the Duke of York
1 March	St David's Day (in Wales only)*
10 March	Birthday of the Earl of Wessex
10 March	Commonwealth Day 2008 (second Monday in March each year)
17 March	St Patrick's Day (in Northern Ireland only)†
21 April	Birthday of the Queen
23 April	St George's Day (in England only)*
9 May	Europe Day‡
2 June	Coronation Day
10 June	Birthday of the Duke of Edinburgh
14 June	The Queen's Official Birthday 2008 (date varies)
17 July	Birthday of the Duchess of Cornwall
15 August	Birthday of the Princess Royal
9 November	Remembrance Sunday 2008 (date varies)
14 November	Birthday of the Prince of Wales
20 November	The Queen's Wedding Day
30 November	St Andrew's Day (in Scotland only)*

The Opening of Parliament by the Queen§
The Prorogation of Parliament by the Queen§

* Where a building has two or more flagstaffs, the appropriate national flag may be flown in addition to the Union Flag, but not in a superior position

† Only the Union Flag should be flown

‡ The Union Flag should fly alongside the European Flag. On government buildings that have only one flagpole, the Union Flag should take precedence

§ Flags are flown whether or not the Queen performs the ceremony in person. Flags are flown only in the Greater London area

FLAGS AT HALF-MAST

Flags are flown at half-mast on the following occasions:

(a)   From the announcement of the death up to the funeral of the sovereign, except on Proclamation Day, when flags are hoisted right up from 11am to sunset

(b)   The funerals of members of the royal family, subject to special commands from the Queen in each case

(c)   The funerals of foreign rulers, subject to special commands from the Queen in each case

(d)   The funerals of prime ministers and ex-prime ministers of the United Kingdom, subject to special commands from the Queen in each case

(e)   Other occasions by special command of the Queen

On occasions when days for flying flags coincide with days for flying flags at half-mast, the following rules are observed. Flags are flown at full mast:

(a)   although a member of the royal family, or a near relative of the royal family, may be lying dead, unless special commands be received from the Queen to the contrary

(b)   although it may be the day of the funeral of a foreign ruler

If the body of a very distinguished subject is lying at a government office, the flag may fly at half-mast on that office until the body has left (provided it is a day on which the flag would fly) and then the flag is to be hoisted right up. On all other government buildings the flag will fly as usual.

THE ROYAL STANDARD

The Royal Standard is hoisted only when the Queen is actually present in the building, and never when she is passing in procession.

FOOD AND DRINK

ALCOHOL

WINE LABELS BY QUALITY

COUNTRY	TABLE WINE	REGIONAL WINE	QUALITY WINE	TOP QUALITY WINE
France	Vin de Table	Vin de Pays	VDQS (Vin Délimité de Qualité Supérieure)	AOC (Appellation d'Origine Contrôlée)
Italy	Vino da Tavola	IGT (Indicazione Geografica Tipica)	DOC (Denominazione di Origine Controllata)	DOCG (Denominazione di Origine Controllata e Garantita)
Germany	Deutscher Tafelwein	Landwein	QbA (Qualitätswein bestimmter Anbaugebiete)	QmP (Qualitätswein mit Prädikat)
Spain	Vino de Mesa	Vino de la Tierra	DO (Denominacién de Origen)	DOC (Denominacién de Origen Calcificada)
Portugal	Vinho de Mesa	Vinho Regional	IPR (Indicacao de Proveniencia Regulamentada)	DOC (Denominacao de Origem Controlada)

COCKTAILS

The International Bartenders Association divides cocktails into four categories: before dinner cocktails, long drinks, fancy drinks and after dinner cocktails.

COCKTAIL	INGREDIENTS
Bellini	Sparkling wine, peach purée
Bloody Mary	Vodka, tomato juice, lemon juice, Worcester sauce, salt and pepper
Buck's Fizz	Champagne, orange juice, grenadine
Cuba Libre	Rum, lime juice, cola

Daiquiri	Rum, lemon juice, sugar
Grasshopper	Crème de menthe, white crème de cacao, whipping cream
Harvey Wallbanger	Vodka, Galliano, orange juice
Long Island Ice Tea	Vodka, gin, tequila, rum, Cointreau, lemon juice, syrup, cola
Manhattan	Rye whisky, sweet vermouth, bitters, maraschino cherry
Margarita	Tequila, lemon juice, Curacao, salt
Martini (dry)	Gin, dry vermouth, olive
Pina Colada	Rum, pineapple juice, coconut milk, cream, sugar
Sex on the Beach	Vodka, peach schnapps, orange juice, cranberry juice
Tequila Sunrise	Tequila, orange juice, grenadine
White Russian	Vodka, coffee liqueur, cream

CALORIES IN ALCOHOL

Bitter, ale, lager and cider values are for half a pint (284ml), wine and champagne – 125ml, spirits – 25ml, alcopop – 275ml. All figures shown below are average amounts and can vary.

DRINK	ALCOHOL BY VOLUME (%)	UNITS	CALORIES
Alcopop	5	1.4	200
Ale	5–6	1.7	80
Bitter	4.2	1.2	91
Brandy	40	1	52
Champagne	12	1.5	89
Cider	6.2	1.8	95
Gin	40	1	56
Lager	4.7	1.3	85
Port	40	1	79
Rum	40	1	58
Sherry	40	1	58
Tequila	40	1	160
Vodka	40	1	55
Whisky	40	1	64
Wine (red) 125ml	12	1.5	85
Wine (white) 125ml	12	1.5	83

HEALTHY EATING

WATER-SOLUBLE VITAMINS

Vitamins are organic compounds, so called because they are vital to life and are essential in small amounts. Care must be taken in cooking to preserve the water-soluble vitamins.

VITAMIN	FUNCTION	SOURCES IN FOOD
C	Maintains connective tissue such as skin and gums; antioxidant	Potatoes; green vegetables; fruit, especially citrus
B1 (Thiamine)	Releases energy from carbohydrate	Milk, wholemeal bread and cereals; meat, especially offal
B2 (Riboflavin)	Utilises energy from food	Dairy produce; yeast; meat, especially liver
B3 (Niacin)	Utilises energy from food	Wholegrain and cereals; fish; meat, especially liver
B6 (Pyridoxine)	Metabolises amino acids and formation of haemoglobin	Occurs widely; especially in wholegrain cereals, meats, fish and eggs
B12	Maintains growth and metabolism; aids the synthesis of red blood cells	Offal; fish; eggs; dairy products
Folic acid	Maintains heart health; helps develop healthy foetuses in pregnant women	Offal; green leafy vegetables; fortified bread and cereals

FAT-SOLUBLE VITAMINS

VITAMIN	FUNCTION	SOURCES IN FOOD
A (Retinol)	Maintains healthy skin and tissues; aids resistance to decease and light perception	Fish liver oil, offal; eggs, carrots, green and yellow vegetables; margarine*
D	Controls and maintains calcium absorption, healthy bones and teeth	Fatty fish; eggs; butter; margarine*
E	Protects cell membranes; antioxidant	Plant sources, especially wheat germ and green vegetables
K	Aids blood clotting	Green vegetables; egg yolk; liver

* Margarine is fortified by law

FRUIT AND VEGETABLES IN SEASON

MONTH	VEGETABLES	FRUIT
January	Artichokes (Jerusalem), Brussels sprouts, cabbages, leeks, onions, parsnips, potatoes	Pears, rhubarb
February	Artichokes (Jerusalem), Brussels sprouts, cabbages, chicory, endive, greens, leeks, onions, potatoes, swede	Rhubarb
March	Broccoli, cabbages, chicory, greens, leeks,	Rhubarb
April	Broccoli, cabbages, cauliflower, greens, lettuce, radishes, sea kale, sorrel	Rhubarb
May	Asparagus, carrots, cauliflower, lettuce, radishes, rocket, sea kale, sorrel, watercress	Rhubarb
June	Asparagus, broad beans, carrots, cauliflower, lettuce, peas, radishes, sorrel, watercress	Cherries, gooseberries, rhubarb, strawberries
July	Artichokes (globe), beetroot, French beans, garlic, kohlrabi, pak choi, peas, potatoes, radishes, spinach, tomatoes	Blackcurrants, cherries, gooseberries, raspberries, redcurrants, strawberries
August	Artichokes (globe), aubergines, beans, beetroot, cabbages, cauliflower, chard, courgettes, cucumber, fennel, garlic, kohlrabi, onions, peas, potatoes, radishes, spinach, sweetcorn, tomatoes, watercress	Apricots, blackberries, blackcurrants, blueberries, nectarines, peaches, plums, raspberries, redcurrants
September	Artichokes (globe), aubergines, beans, beetroot, broccoli, cabbages, carrots, cauliflower, chard, chillies, courgettes, fennel, garlic, kale, kohlrabi, lamb's lettuce, onions, pak choi, peppers, pumpkins, rocket, spinach, sweetcorn, tomatoes, watercress	Apples, blackberries, blueberries, greengages, peaches, pears, plums
October	Beetroot, broccoli, cabbages, carrots, cauliflower, celeriac, celery, courgettes, kale, kohlrabi, leeks, onions, peppers, potatoes, pumpkins, spinach, tomatoes, turnips	Apples, grapes, pears, quinces, raspberries
November	Artichoke (Jerusalem), beetroot, cabbages, carrots, celeriac, celery, chicory, endive, greens, kohlrabi, leeks, lettuce, onions, parsnips, potatoes, pumpkins, swede, turnips	Apples, pears, quinces, raspberries
December	Artichoke (Jerusalem), Brussels sprouts, carrots, greens, kale, leeks, onions, parsnips, potatoes, swede, turnips	Apples

POPULAR DIETS

DIET	RULES
Atkins	Low amounts of carbohydrate-rich food allowed, high intake of protein
Blood Type	Recommended foods allocated according to blood type
Hay diet	Carbohydrates and protein only eaten in separate meal
Low GI	Low glycaemic index foods
Macrobiotic	Daily intake: 30% vegetables, 50% whole grains, 10% soup, 5% fruit, 5% seaweed
Ornish	Vegetarian, less than 10% of calories as fat, high in fibre, no calorie restrictions
Raw foods	Foods that have not been heated over the specified temperature
Single foods	Single type of food at a particular time each day or an unlimited number of times for a week
The Zone	A mixture of carbohydrate, fat and low-fat protein at each meal to control insulin level
Weight Watchers	Foods allocated points according to a scoring system, a certain amount of points is allowed each day

HEALTHY WEIGHT CHART

The table below can be used to find out the ideal weight for any height. Alternatively, for metric units, calculate your Body Mass Index (BMI) using:

$$BMI = \frac{Weight\ (kg)}{Height\ (m^2)}$$

The World Health Organisation recommends that a healthy BMI is between 18.5 and 24.9, less than 18.4 is underweight, and over 30 is obese.

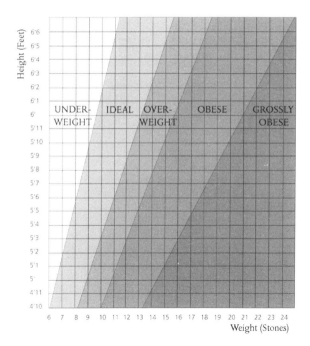

TYPES OF CHEESE

CHEESE	COUNTRY	CHARACTERISTICS
Brie	France	Soft, cow's milk, downy rind
Camembert	France	Soft, cow's milk, downy rind
Cheddar	England	Hard, cow's milk, white to yellow
Dolcelatte	Italy	Semi-soft, cow's milk, mould-ripened, blue/green veined
Edam	The Netherlands	Semi-hard, skimmed cow's milk, mild, red wax rind
Emmenthal	Switzerland	Hard, cow's milk, creamy
Gorgonzola	Italy	Semi-hard, cow's milk, mould-ripened, blue/green veined
Gouda	The Netherlands	Semi-hard, cow's milk, mild, yellow wax rind
Gruyère	Switzerland	Hard, cow's milk, small holes
Feta	Greece	Soft, ewe's or goat's milk, salty
Lancashire	England	Hard, cow's milk, white, crumbly
Leicester	England	Hard, cow's milk, white, crumbly
Manchego	Spain	Semi-hard, ewe's milk, mild or sharp
Munster	Germany	Semi-soft, cow's milk, bacteria-ripened
Parmesan	Italy	Very hard, cow's milk, bacteria-ripened, long cure
Port Salut	France	Semi-soft, cow's milk, yellow
Roquefort	France	Semi-hard, ewe's milk, blue veined
Stilton	England	Semi-hard, cow's milk, mould-ripened, blue veined

CULINARY TERMS

TERM	DEFINITION
Al dente	Of pasta that is firm when bitten (*trans.* to the tooth)
Aperitif	Alcoholic drink taken before a meal
Blanch	To boil food in water briefly
Cacciatore	Chicken or veal cooked with tomatoes, mushrooms, onions and herbs
Canapé	Appetiser, small piece of bread or toast with savoury topping
Chasseur	Sauce made with mushrooms, white wine, shallots and herbs
Entrée	Dish served before the main course
Flambé	To cover food with alcohol and ignite before serving
Florentine	Cooked in the style of Florence, usually with spinach
Fricassée	Meat diced and cooked in gravy
Haute cuisine	Fine cuisine, elaborately prepared
Hors d'oeuvre	Appetiser served before a meal
Lyonnaise	Cooked in the style of Lyons, with onions and usually with potatoes
En papillote	Food cooked and served in parchment paper
Passata	Italian sauce made from sieved tomatoes
Provençale	Cooked in the style of Provence, with tomatoes, onions, garlic and olive oil
Roux	Cooked mixture of flour and fat used to thicken sauces
Sauté	To quickly fry in a shallow pan
Tapas	Spanish appetisers, can make up a whole meal
Tikka	Meat marinated in yoghurt and spices, cooked in a clay oven
Timbale	Meat or fish cooked in a cup-shaped mould or shell

SHOOTING SEASONS

DEER

The statutory close seasons for deer are listed below, it is illegal to shoot deer during this time.

SPECIES	SEX	ENGLAND/WALES/ NORTHERN IRELAND	SCOTLAND
Red	Stags	1 May–31 Jul	21 Oct–30 Jun
	Hinds	1 Mar–31 Oct	16 Feb–20 Oct
Fallow	Bucks	1 May–31 Jul	1 May–31 Jul
	Does	1 Mar–31 Oct	16 Feb–20 Oct
Sika	Stags	1 May–31 Jul	21 Oct–30 Jun
	Hinds	1 Mar–31 Oct	16 Feb–20 Oct
Roe	Bucks	1 Nov–31 Mar	21 Oct–31 Mar
	Does	1 Mar–31 Oct	1 Apr–20 Oct
Red/Sika	Stags	1 May–31 Jul	21 Oct–30 Jun
Hybrids	Hinds	1 Mar–31 Oct	16 Feb–20 Oct

GAME

It is an offence to kill or take game birds between the following dates and on Sundays and Christmas Day (in England and Wales)

GAME BIRD (COMMON NAME)	CLOSE SEASONS
Black game (black grouse)	10 Dec–20 Aug
Capercaillie*	1 Feb–30 Sept
Grouse (red grouse and ptarmigan)	10 Dec–12 Aug
Partridges (grey partridge and red-legged partridge)	1 Feb–1 Sep
Pheasants	1 Feb–1 Oct
Snipe, Common	1 Feb–11 Aug
Woodcock†	1 Feb–30 Sept

* Capercaillie are now fully protected in Scotland;

† The close season for woodcock is different in Scotland (1 Feb to 31 Aug)

GEOGRAPHY

THE EARTH

DIMENSIONS

Surface area = 510,069,120 km^2 (196,938,800 miles^2), of which water makes up 70.92 per cent and land 29.08 per cent

Equatorial diameter = 12,756.27 km (7,926.38 miles)

Polar diameter = 12,713.50 km (7,899.80 miles)

Equatorial circumference = 40,075.01 km (24,901.46 miles)

Polar circumference = 40,007.86 km (24,859.73 miles)

Equator = 0°

North Pole = 90° N.

South Pole = 90° S.

Tropic of Cancer = 23°26′ N.

Tropic of Capricorn = 23°26′ S.

Arctic Circle = 66°34′ N.

Antarctic Circle = 66°34′ S.

The Tropics and the Arctic and Antarctic circles are affected by the slow decrease in obliquity of the ecliptic, of about 0.5 arcseconds per year. The effect of this is that the Arctic and Antarctic circles are currently moving towards their respective poles by about 14 metres per year, while the Tropics move towards the Equator by the same amount.

The Earth is divided by geologists into three layers:

Crust	thin outer layer, with an average depth of 24 km/15 miles, although the depth varies widely depending on whether it is under land or sea
Mantle	lies between the crust and the core and is about 2,865 km/1,780 miles thick
Core	extends from the mantle to the Earth's centre and is about 6,964 km/4,327 miles in diameter

THE ATMOSPHERE

The atmosphere is the air or mixture of gases enveloping the Earth. Various layers are identified by scientists, based on rate of temperature change, composition, etc. These are:

Ionosphere (includes the thermosphere)

Mesopause

Mesosphere

Stratopause

Stratosphere (the upper atmosphere)

Tropopause
Troposphere (the lower atmosphere)
(Boundary layer – up to 2 km)
Earth's surface

Most weather conditions form in the troposphere, and this is also the layer where most pollutants released into the atmosphere by human activity accumulate. The stratosphere is the layer in which most atmospheric ozone is found.

The component gases of the atmosphere are:

GAS	% BY VOL.
Nitrogen	78.10
Oxygen	20.95
Argon	0.934
Carbon dioxide	0.031
Neon	0.00182
Helium	0.00052
Methane	0.00020
Krypton	0.00011
Hydrogen	0.00005
Nitrous oxide	0.00005
Ozone	0.00004
Xenon	0.000009

ATMOSPHERIC POLLUTION

The Framework Convention on Climate Change was adopted by 153 states at the UN Conference on Environment and Development (UNCED) at Rio de Janiero, Brazil, in 1992. It is intended to reduce the risks of global warming by limiting 'greenhouse' gas emissions. Progress towards the Convention's targets is assessed at regular conferences. Under the Kyoto Protocol, adopted in 1997, industrialised countries agreed to legally binding targets for cutting emissions of greenhouse gases by 5.2 per cent below 1990 levels by 2008–2012. EU members agreed to an 8 per cent reduction and UK's target is a 12.5 per cent cut.

The six main 'greenhouse' gases identified by the convention are:
  carbon dioxide
  methane
  nitrous oxide
  hydrofluorocarbons (HFCs)
  perfluorocarbons (PFCs)
  sulphur hexafluoride (SF_6)

GEOLOGICAL TIME

PRECAMBRIAN ERA *c.*4,600 – *c.*542 million years ago
Archean	Earth uninhabited
Proterozoic	First primitive life forms, e.g. algae, bacteria

PALAEOZOIC ERA ('ancient life') *c.*542 – *c.*251 million years ago
Cambrian	Mainly sandstones, slate and shales; limestones in Scotland. First shelled fossils and invertebrates
Ordovician	Mainly shales and mudstones, e.g. in north Wales. First fishes
Silurian	Shales, mudstones and some limestones, found mostly in Wales and southern Scotland
Devonian	Old red sandstone, shale, limestone and slate, e.g. in south Wales and the West Country
Carboniferous	Coal-bearing rocks, millstone grit, limestone and shale. First traces of land-living creatures
Permian	Marls, sandstones and clays. Glaciations in southern continents. First reptiles

MESOZOIC ERA ('middle forms of life') *c.*251 – *c.*65.5 million years ago
Triassic	Mostly sandstone, e.g. in the West Midlands. First mammals
Jurassic	Mainly limestones and clays, typically displayed in the Jura mountains, and in England in a NE–SW belt from Lincolnshire and the Wash to the Severn and the Dorset coast. First birds
Cretaceous	Mainly chalk, clay and sands, e.g. in Kent and Sussex

CENOZOIC ERA ('recent life') from *c.*65.5 million years ago

TERTIARY
Palaeocene	Emergence of new forms of life, including existing species
Eocene	Emergence of first modern mammals
Oligocene	Fossils of a few still existing species
Miocene	Fossil remains show a balance of existing and extinct species
Pliocene	Fossil remains show a majority of still existing species

QUATERNARY
Pleistocene	Glaciations and interglacials
	Majority of remains are those of still existing species
Holocene	Present, post-glacial period
	Existing species only, except for a few exterminated by humans

EARTHQUAKES

Movements on or in the Earth generate seismic waves. These can be measured in a variety of ways, and there are a number of different scales for comparing the relative size of earthquakes based on seismic waves, usually called seismic magnitudes. The nature of seismic waves means that any one earthquake can have many different seismic magnitudes. The main magnitude scales are:

NAME	PERIOD OF MEASUREMENT (IN SECONDS)
Richter magnitude	0.1–1.0
body wave magnitude	1.0–5.0
surface wave magnitude	20
moment magnitude	>200

The point of initiation of an earthquake is known as the hypocentre (usually given in terms of latitude, longitude, and depth below the surface). The epicentre is the surface projection of the hypocentre.

RICHTER SCALE

Named after Charles Richter, who invented seismic magnitude scales in the 1930s.

MAGNITUDE	INTENSITY
1	Detectable only by instruments
2	Barely detectable, even near epicentre
3	Similar to vibrations from a heavy goods vehicle
4–5	Detectable within 32 km/20 miles of the epicentre; possible slight damage within a small area
6	Moderately destructive
7	Major earthquake
8	Great earthquake

MODIFIED MERCALLI SCALE

Used mainly in Japan and most of the former Soviet republics.

MAGNITUDE	INTENSITY
I	Detectable only by instruments
II	Felt by a few people at rest
III	Felt noticeably indoors; standing cars may rock
IV	Felt generally indoors; sleepers woken
V	Felt generally; plaster falls; dishes and windows broken
VI	Felt by all; chimneys and plaster damaged; objects upset
VII	Everyone runs outdoors; felt in moving cars; walls crack
VIII	General alarm; weak structures damaged; walls collapse
IX	Weak structures destroyed; ground fissured and cracked
X	Most buildings destroyed; ground badly cracked; water slopped over river banks
XI	Few buildings survive; broad fissures in ground; landslides
XII	Total destruction; waves seen on ground; objects thrown into air

THE WORLD'S MOST DESTRUCTIVE EARTHQUAKES

(by number of fatalities, Richter scale)

DATE	LOCATION	FATALITIES	MAGNITUDE
23 January 1556	China, Shansi	830,000	~8
27 July 1976	China, Tangshan	255,000*	7.5
9 August 1138	Syria, Aleppo	230,000	Unknown
22 May 1927	China, near Xining	200,000	7.9
22 December 856	Iran, Damghan	200,000	Unknown

* Official number; real figure possibly as high as 650,000

WEATHER

WIND FORCE MEASURES

The Beaufort Scale of wind force is used internationally in communicating weather conditions. Devised originally by Admiral Sir Francis Beaufort in 1805 as a scale of 0–12, it was extended to Force 17 by the US Weather Bureau in the 1950s. Each scale number represents a certain strength or velocity of wind at 10 m (33 ft) above ground in the open.

SCALE NO.	WIND FORCE	MPH	KNOTS
0	Calm	0–1	0–1
1	Light air	1–3	1–3
2	Slight breeze	4–7	4–6
3	Gentle breeze	8–12	7–10
4	Moderate breeze	13–18	11–16
5	Fresh breeze	19–24	17–21
6	Strong breeze	25–31	22–27
7	High wind	32–38	28–33
8	Gale	39–46	34–40
9	Strong gale	47–54	41–47
10	Whole gale	55–63	48–55
11	Storm	64–72	56–63
12	Hurricane	73–82	64–71
13	—	83–92	72–80
14	—	93–103	81–89
15	—	104–114	90–99
16	—	115–125	100–108
17	—	126–136	109–118

WIND CHILL FACTOR

Wind chill is the apparent temperature felt on exposed skin due to the effect of wind speed. The laws of thermodynamics state that any object at a temperature greater than the air around it will lose heat. The greater the difference in temperature between the object and the surrounding air, the faster the rate at which energy is transferred.

Wind chill can be calculated using the following equation:

$$T_{wc} = 13.12 + 0.6215\,T_d - 11.37\,V^{0.16} + 0.3965\,T_d V^{0.16}$$

where T_{wc} is the wind chill index based on the Celsius scale, T_d is the air temperature in °C and V is the air speed in km/h (measured at a constant height of 10m). This calculation produces the following wind chill values:

		Temperature (°C)										
		0	−1	−2	−3	−4	−5	−10	−15	−20–	−25	−30
	6	−2	−3	−4	−5	−7	−8	−14	−19	−25	−31	−37
	8	−3	−4	−5–	−6	−7	−9	−14	−20	−26	−32	−38
	10	−3	−5	−6	−7	−8	−9	−15	−21	−27	−33	−39
	15	−4	−6	−7	−8	−9	−11	−17	−23	−29	−35	−41
	20	−5	−7	−8	−8	−10	−12	−18	−24	−30	−37	−43
	25	−6	−7	−8	−10	−11	−12	−19	−25	−32	−38	−44
	30	−6	−8	−9	−10	−12	−13	−20	−26	−33	−39	−46
	35	−7	−8	−10	−11	−12	−14	−20	−27	−33	−40	−47
	40	−7	−9	−10	−11	−13	−14	−21	−27	−34	−41	−48
	45	−8	−9	−10	−12	−13	−15	−21	−28	−35	−42	−48
	50	−8	−10	−11	−12	−14	−15	−22	−29	−35	−42	−49
	55	−8	−10	−11	−13	−14	−15	−22	−29	−36	−43	−50
	60	−9	−10	−12	−13	−14	−16	−23	−30	−26	−43	−50
	65	−9	−10	−12	−13	−15	−16	−23	−30	−37	−44	−51
	70	−9	−11	−12	−14	−15	−16	−23	−20	−37	−44	−51

Wind Speed (km/h)

CLOUD TYPES

Clouds comprise suspended particles of water or ice, or both. The water is condensed from air which rises into levels of lower atmospheric pressure, expands and cools to form water drops. These can remain liquid to temperatures of -30°C but below this temperature start to freeze to ice crystals. Below -40°C, clouds consist of ice crystals alone.

Clouds are classified according to the height of their base from the ground and to their shape. The basic cloud types are:

cirrus (a filament of hair)	high wispy ice clouds
stratus (a layer)	laminar, e.g. flat
cumulus (a heap or pile)	rounded, with strong vertical structure
nimbus (a rain cloud)	precipitating

The original classification scheme, devised by an English pharmacist, Luke Howard, in 1803, has been expanded to include ten cloud types:

TYPE (BASE HEIGHT ABOVE GROUND LEVEL)	WATER PHASE	DISTINCTIVE FEATURES
HIGH CLOUDS (over 5,000 m/16,500 ft)		
Cirrus (Ci)	ice	mares tails
Cirrostratus (Cs)	ice	halo cloud
Cirrocumulus (Cc)	ice or mixed	mackerel sky
MIDDLE CLOUDS (2,000 m/6,500 ft to 7,000 m/23,000 ft)		
Altostratus (As)	mixed or ice	overcast
Altocumulus (Ac)	liquid or mixed	widespread, cotton balls
LOW CLOUDS (below 2,000 m/6,500 ft)		
Nimbostratus (Ns)	mixed or ice	low, dark grey
Stratus (St)	liquid	hazy layer, like high fog
Stratocumulus (Sc)	liquid or mixed	widespread, heavy rolls
VERTICAL CLOUDS (1,000 m/3,000 ft to 5,000 m/16,500 ft)		
Cumulus (Cu)	liquid	fluffy, billowy
Cumulonimbus (Cb)	mixed	flat bottom, anvil-shaped top

WORLD GEOGRAPHICAL STATISTICS

OCEANS

AREA	KM^2	MILES^2
Pacific	155,557,000	59,270,000
Atlantic	76,762,000	29,638,000
Indian	68,556,000	26,467,000
Southern*	20,327,000	7,848,300
Arctic	14,056,000	5,427,000

* 2000 the International Hydrographic Organisation approved the description of the 20,327,000 km^2 (7,848,300 miles^2) of circum-Antarctic waters up to 60°S. as the Southern Ocean. The division by the Equator of the Pacific into the North and South Pacific and the Atlantic into the North and South Atlantic makes a total of seven oceans.

SEAS

AREA	KM^2	MILES^2
South China	2,974,600	1,148,500
Caribbean	2,515,900	971,400
Mediterranean	2,509,900	969,100
Bering	2,261,000	873,000
Gulf of Mexico	1,507,600	582,100
Okhotsk	1,392,000	537,500
Japan	1,012,900	391,100
Hudson Bay	730,100	281,900
East China	664,600	256,600
Andaman	564,880	218,100
Black Sea	507,900	196,100
Red Sea	453,000	174,900
North Sea	427,100	164,900
Baltic Sea	382,000	147,500
Yellow Sea	294,000	113,500
Persian Gulf	230,000	88,800

THE CONTINENTS

There are six geographic continents, although America is often divided politically into North, Central and South America.

AREA	KM^2	MILES^2
Asia	43,998,000	16,988,000
America*	41,918,000	16,185,000
Africa	29,800,000	11,506,000
Antarctica	13,209,000	5,100,000
Europe†	9,699,000	3,745,000
Australia	7,618,493	2,941,526

* North and Central America have a combined area of 24,255,000 km^2 (9,365,000 miles^2)

† Includes 5,571,000 km^2 (2,151,000 miles^2) of former USSR territory, including the Baltic states, Belarus, Moldova, the Ukraine and part of Russia west of the Ural mountains and Kazakhstan west of the Ural river. European Turkey (24,378 km^2/9,412 miles^2) comprises territory to the west and north of the Bosporus and the Dardanelles

LARGEST ISLANDS

AREA	KM^2	MILES^2
Greenland	2,175,500	840,000
New Guinea	792,500	306,000
Borneo	725,450	280,100
Madagascar	587,041	226,674
Baffin Island	507,451	195,928
Sumatra	427,350	165,000
Honshu	227,413	87,805
Great Britain*	218,077	84,200
Victoria Island	217,292	83,897
Ellesmere Island	196,236	75,767

*Mainland only

LARGEST DESERTS

AREA	KM^2	MILES^2
Sahara	9,000,000	3,500,000
Gobi	1,300,000	500,000
Australian*	1,120,000	460,000
Arabian	1,000,000	385,000
Kalahari	570,000	220,000
Taklimakan Shamo	320,000	125,000

* includes Great Sandy, Gibson, Simpson and Great Victoria

HIGHEST MOUNTAINS

The world's 8,000-metre mountains (with six subsidiary peaks) are all in Asia's Himalaya-Karakoram-Hindu Kush ranges.

	HEIGHT	
	METRES	FEET
Mt Everest (Qomolangma)	8,850	29,035
K2 (Qogir)†	8,611	28,251
Kangchenjunga	8,597	28,208
Lhotse I	8,510	27,923
Makalu I	8,480	27,824
Lhotse Shar (II)	8,400	27,560

† Formerly Godwin-Austin

The culminating summits in the other major mountain ranges are:

MOUNTAIN (by range or country)

	HEIGHT	
	METRES	FEET
Pik Pobedy, Tien Shan	7,439	24,406
Cerro Aconcagua, Andes	6,960	22,834
Mt McKinley (S. Peak), Alaska	6,194	20,320
Kilimanjaro, Tanzania	5,894	19,340
Hkakabo Razi, Myanmar	5,881	19,296
Citlaltépetl, Mexico	5,655	18,555
El'brus (W. Peak), Caucasus	5,642	18,510
Vinson Massif, Antarctica	4,897	16,066
Puncak Jaya, New Guinea	4,884	16,023
Mt Blanc, Alps	4,807	15,771
BRITISH ISLES (by country)		
Ben Nevis, Scotland	1,344	4,406
Snowdon, Wales	1,085	3,559
Carrantuohill, Rep. of Ireland	1,050	3,414
Scafell Pike, England	977	3,210

LARGEST LAKES

The areas of some of these lakes are subject to seasonal variation.

	AREA	
	KM^2	$MILES^2$
Caspian Sea, Iran/Azerbaijan/ Russia/Turkmenistan/Kazakhstan	371,000	143,000
Michigan-Huron, USA/Canada*	117,610	45,300

	AREA	
	KM²	MILES²
Superior, Canada/USA	82,100	31,700
Victoria, Uganda/Tanzania/Kenya	69,500	26,828
Tanganyika, Dem. Rep. of Congo/ Tanzania/Zambia/Burundi	32,900	12,665
Great Bear, Canada	31,328	12,096
Baykal (Baikal), Russia	30,500	11,776
Malawi (Nyasa), Tanzania/Malawi/ Mozambique	28,900	11,150

* Lakes Michigan and Huron are regarded as lobes of the same lake. The Michigan lobe has an area of 57,750 km² (22,300 miles²) and the Huron lobe an area of 59,570 km² (23,000 miles²)

UNITED KINGDOM (by country)

Lough Neagh, Northern Ireland	381.73	147.39
Loch Lomond, Scotland	71.12	27.46
Windermere, England	14.74	5.69
Lake Vyrnwy (artificial), Wales	4.53	1.75
Llyn Tegid (Bala) (natural), Wales	4.38	1.69

DEEPEST LAKES

LAKE	LOCATION	GREATEST DEPTH	
		METRES	FEET
Baikal	Russia	1,637	5,371
Tanganyika	Burundi/Tanzania/Dem. Rep. of Congo/Zambia	1,470	4,825
Caspian Sea	Azerbaijan/Iran/Kazakhstan/Russia/Turkmenistan	1,025	3,363
Malawi	Malawi/Mozambique/Tanzania	706	2,316
Issyk Kul	Kyrgyzstan	702	2,303
Great Slave	Canada	614	2,015
Danau Toba	Indonesia	590	1,936
Hornindalsvastnet	Norway	514	1,686
Sarezskoye Ozero	Tajikistan	505	1,657
Tahoe	California/Nevada, USA	501	1,645
Lago Argentina	Argentina	500	1,640
Lac Kivu	Rwanda/Dem. Rep. of Congo	480	1,574
Quesnel	Canada	475	1,558

All these lakes would be sufficiently deep to submerge the Empire State Building – in the case of Lake Baikal, more than four times over.

LONGEST RIVERS

	LENGTH	
	KM	MILES
Nile, Africa	6,725	4,180
Amazon, S. America	6,448	4,007
Yangtze-Kiang (Chang Jiang), China	6,380	3,964
Mississippi-Missouri-Red Rock, N. America	5,970	3,710
Yenisey-Angara, Mongolia/Russia	5,536	3,440
Huang He (Yellow River), China	5,463	3,395
BRITISH ISLES (by country)		
Shannon, Rep. of Ireland	386	240
Severn, Britain	354	220
Thames, England	346	215
Tay, Scotland	188	117
Clyde, Scotland	158	98.5

HIGHEST WATERFALLS

	TOTAL DROP		GREATEST SINGLE LEAP	
WATERFALL, RIVER AND LOCATION	METRES	FEET	METRES	FEET
Saltó Angel, Carrao Auyán Tepuí, Venezuela	979	3,212	807	2,648
Tugela, Tugela, Natal, S. Africa	948	3,110	410	1,350
Utigård, Jostedal Glacier, Norway	800	2,625	600	1,970
Mongefossen, Monge, Norway	774	2,540	—	—
Gocta, Cocahuayco, Peru	771	2,531	—	—
Mutarazi, Zambezi, Zimbabwe	762	2,499	479	1,572
Yosemite, Yosemite Creek, USA	739	2,425	435	1,430
Østre Mardøla Foss, Mardals, Norway*	655	2,149	296	974
Tyssestrengene, Tysso, Norway*	646	2,120	289	948
Cuquenán, Arabopó, Venezuela	610	2,000	—	—
Sutherland, Arthur, NZ	580	1,904	248	815

* cascades

LANGUAGE

MOST WIDELY SPOKEN LANGUAGES

LANGUAGE	SPEAKERS (THOUSANDS)
1. Mandarin Chinese	1,125,000
2. English	350,000
3. Spanish	225,000
4. Hindi	180,000
5. Bengali	180,000
6. Russian	175,000
7. Arabic	165,000
8. Japanese	120,000
9. German	120,000
10. Portuguese	155,000

PUNCTUATION MARKS AND DIACRITICS

The list below gives the names of the punctuation marks and accents in common usage.

,	comma
;	semicolon
:	colon
.	full stop
?	question mark
!	exclamation mark
'	apostrophe
' '	single quotation marks
" "	double quotation marks
( )	parentheses
[ ]	square brackets
< >	angle brackets
{ }	curly brackets
-	hyphen
—	dash
{	brace
&	ampersand
*	asterisk
...	mark of omission/ellipsis
á	acute accent
à	grave accent
â	circumflex
ç	cedilla
ë	umlaut (diaresis)
ñ	tilde
s	caron
å	ångström

COLLECTIVE NOUNS FOR ANIMALS

The following terms for groups of animals are derived from medieval bestiaries.

Ants	army, column, state, swarm
Apes	shrewdness
Baboons	troop
Badgers	cete, colony
Bears	sloth
Beavers	colony
Bees	cluster, erst, hive, swarm
Budgerigars	chatter
Camels	caravan, flock
Caterpillars	army
Cats	chowder, clowder, cluster
Chickens	brood, clutch, peep
Crows	clan, hover, murder
Dogs	cowardice, kennel, pack
Dolphins	pod, school
Doves	dole, flight, prettying
Eagles	convocation
Eels	swarm
Falcons	cast
Ferrets	business, cast, fesynes
Flamingos	flurry, regiment, skein

Flies	business, cloud, scraw, swarm
Foxes	earth, lead, skulk
Frogs	army, colony
Geese	gaggle
Giraffes	corps, herd, troop
Goldfinch	charm, chattering, chirp, drum
Goldfish	troubling
Grasshoppers	cloud
Greyhounds	brace, leash, pack
Grouse	brood, covey, pack
Hares	down, drove, husk, lie, trip
Hawks	cast
Hedgehogs	array
Herons	scattering, sedge, siege
Herring	army, gleam, shoal
Ibis	crowd
Jellyfish	brood, smuck
Lapwings	deceit, desert
Larks	exultation
Leopards	leap
Lions	flock, pride, sawt, souse, troop
Mackerel	school, shoal
Magpies	tiding, tittering
Mice	nest
Moles	company, labour, movement, mumble
Monkeys	troop
Mules	barren, cartload, pack, span
Nightingales	match, puddling, watch
Otters	bevy, family
Owls	parliament, stare
Partridges	covey
Peacocks	muster
Penguins	colony, rookery

Pheasants	brook, ostentation, pride, nye
Piglets	farrow
Pigs	litter, herd, sounder
Plover	congregation, flight, stand, wing
Quail	bevy, covey
Rabbits	bury, colony, nest, warren
Raccoons	nursery
Rats	colony
Ravens	unkindness
Rhinoceros	crash
Rooks	building, clamour, parliament
Sardines	family
Seals	harem, herd, pod, rookery
Snakes	den, pit
Snipe	walk, whisper, wish, wisp
Sparrows	host, surration, quarrel
Spiders	cluster, clutter
Squirrels	drey
Starlings	chattering, crowd, murmuration
Swans	bank, bevy, game, herd, squadron, teeme, wedge, whiteness
Thrush	mutation
Tigers	ambush
Toads	knab, knot
Trout	hover
Turkeys	dule, raffle, rafter
Turtle Doves	pitying
Turtles	bale, dole
Wasps	herd, nest, pladge
Whales	colony, gam, herd, pod, school
Woodcocks	covey, fall, flight, plump
Woodpeckers	descent

NAMES OF MALE, FEMALE AND YOUNG ANIMALS

ANIMAL	MALE	FEMALE	YOUNG
Ape	male	female	baby
Bear	boar	sow	cub
Camel	bull	cow	calf
Chicken	rooster	hen	chick, pullet (hen), cockrell (rooster)
Deer	buck, stag	doe	fawn
Donkey	jack, jackass	jennet, jenny	colt, foal
Elephant	bull	cow	calf
Ferret	hob	jill	kit
Fox	reynard	vixen	kit, cub, pup
Giraffe	bull	doe	calf
Goat	buck, billy	doe, nanny	kid, billy
Gorilla	male	female	infant
Hamster	buck	doe	pup
Hippopotamus	bull	cow	calf
Horse	stallion, stud	mare, dam	foal, colt (male), filly (female)
Human	man	woman	baby, infant, toddler
Lion	lion	lioness	cub
Louse	male	female	nymph
Mouse	buck	doe	pup, pinkie, kitten
Ostrich	cock	hen	chick
Pig	boar	sow	piglet, shoat, farrow
Rhinoceros	bull	cow	calf
Seal	bull	cow	pup
Sheep	buck, ram	ewe, dam	lamb, lambkin, cosset
Turkey	tom	hen	poult
Turtle	male	female	hatchling
Whale	bull	cow	calf
Wolf	dog	bitch	pup, whelp
Zebra	stallion	mare	colt, foal

LATIN FLOWER AND PLANT NAMES

Ash	*Fraxinus excelsior*
Aspen	*Populus tremula*
Basil	*Ocimum*
Bellflower	*Campanula*
Bramble	*Rubus*
Busy Lizzie	*Impatiens walleriana*
Carnation	*Dianthus*
Cypress	*Cupressus*
Daffodil	*Narcissus sylvestris*
Dandelion	*Leontodon*
Fennel	*Anethum elaterium*
Fern	*Filix*
Foxglove	*Digitalis*
Geranium, rose	*Geranium roseum*
Grass	*Gramen*
Holly	*Ilex*
Honeysuckle	*Lanicera caprifolium*
Ivy	*Hedera helix*
Lavender	*Lavandula spica*
Lilac	*Lilac vulgaris*
Lily of the Valley	*Convallaria majalis*
Peppermint	*Mentha piperita*
Poppy	*Papaver*
Prickly pear	*Cactus opuntia*
Snapdragon	*Antirrhinum majus*
Snowdrop	*Galanthus nivalis*
Sweet Pea	*Lathyrus odoratus*
Sweet William	*Dianthus barbatus*
Sunflower	*Helianthus annuus*
Thistle	*Carduus*
Tulip	*Tulipia*
Weeping willow	*Salix babylonica*

LATIN FRUIT AND VEGETABLE NAMES

Apple	*Malus sylvestris*
Apricot	*Prunus armeniaca*
Avocado	*Persea americana*
Aubergine	*Solanum melongena*
Beetroot	*Beta vulgaris*
Blackberry	*Rubus fruticosis*
Blackcurrant	*Ribes nigrum*
Broccoli	*Brassica oleracea*
Clementine	*Citrus reticulata*
Coconut	*Cocos nucifera*
Cranberry	*Oxycoccus macrocarpus*
Cucumber	*Cucumis sativus*
Garlic	*Alliumsativum*
Grape	*Vitis vinifera*
Grapefruit	*Citrus paradisi*
Kiwi fruit	*Actinidia deliciosa*
Lemon	*Citrus limon*
Lettuce	*Lactuca sativa*
Lime	*Citrus aurantifolia*
Mango	*Mangifera indica*
Mushroom	*Agaricus campestris*
Olive	*Olea europaea*
Onion	*Allium cepa*
Orange	*Citrus sinensis*
Pea	*Pisum sativum*
Peach	*Prunus persica*
Pear	*Pyrus cummunis*
Pepper	*Capsicum annuum*
Pineapple	*Ananas comosus*
Plum	*Prunus domestica*
Pomegranate	*Punica granatum*
Potato	*Solanum tuberosum*
Pumpkin	*Cucurbita pepo*
Raspberry	*Rubus idaeus*
Runner bean	*Phaseolus coccineus*
Satsuma	*Citrus nobilis*
Tomato	*Lycopersicon esculentum*
Watermelon	*Citrullus lanatus*

COMMON LATIN PHRASES

a priori from what was before

ad absurdum to the point of absurdity

ad hoc for this special purpose

ad hominem appealing to feelings rather than reason

ad infinitum without limit

ad nauseam to a tedious extent

addenda items to be added

affidavit a sworn written statement usable as evidence in court

alma mater old school or college

alter ego other self

annus horribilis a bad year

annus mirabilis a wonderful year

ante bellum before the war

ars gratia artis art for art's sake

bona fide (adjective) genuine

carpe diem seize the day

casus belli the circumstances justifying war

caveat emptor let the buyer beware

circa (abbreviated *c* and followed by a date) about

cogito, ergo sum I think, therefore I am (Descartes)

compos mentis sane

cui bono? who benefits?

curriculum vitae a summary of a person's career

de facto in fact (especially in contradiction to *de jure*)

de jure by right (especially in contradiction to *de facto*)

deus ex machina a contrived event that resolves a problem at the last moment

dramatis personae the list of characters in a play

ecce homo behold the man

ego consciousness of one's own identity

ergo therefore

et alii (abbreviated *et al*) and others

ex cathedra (of a pronouncement) formally, with official authority

fiat let it be done

habeas corpus you may have the body (the opening words of a prerogative writ requiring a person holding another person to bring that person before a court)

ibidem (abbreviated *ibid* in citations of books, etc) in the same place

in absentia while absent

in extremis near death

in flagrante delicto in the very act of committing an offence

in loco parentis in place of a parent

in memoriam in memory

in situ in its original situation

in vino veritas in wine there is truth

in vitro outside the living body and in an artificial environment

in vivo happening within a living organism

infra below or on a later page

inter alia among other things

ipso facto by that very fact

magna cum laude with great honour or distinction

magnum opus great work

mea culpa by my fault (used as an acknowledgment of error)

memento mori remember that you have to die

mens rea guilty mind

mens sana in corpore sano a sound mind in a sound body

modus operandi the manner of working

mutatis mutandis the necessary changes being made

non sequitur it does not follow

passim in various places (in a quoted piece of work)

per annum per year

per ardua ad astra through difficulties to the stars

per capita by the head

per centum per hundred

per diem per day

per se taken alone

persona non grata a non-acceptable person

post mortem after death (also figuratively)

prima facie on a first view

pro bono done without charge in the public interest

pro forma for the sake of form

pro rata according to the rate

pro tempore (abbreviated to *pro tem*) for the time being

quid pro quo something for something

quo vadis? where are you going?

quod erat demonstrandum (abbreviated QED) which was to be proved

quod vide (abbreviated *q.v.*) which see

reduction ad absurdum reduction to the absurd (proving the truth of a proposition by proving the falsity of all its alternatives)

sic thus

sic transit gloria mundi thus passes the glory of the world

sine qua non an indispensable condition

status quo the existing condition

stet let it stand

sub judice before a court

tempus fugit time flies

terra firma dry land

terra incognita unknown land

vade mecum a constant companion

veni, vedi, vici I came, I saw, I conquered (Caesar)

verbatim exactly as said

vice versa the order being reversed

vox populi voice of the people

PHOBIAS

Acrophobia	fear of heights
Agoraphobia	fear of open spaces
Ailurophobia	fear of cats
Algophobia	fear of pain
Androphobia	fear of men
Anthophobia	fear of flowers
Anthropophobia	fear of people
Apiphobia	fear of bees
Arachnophobia	fear of spiders
Ataxiaphobia	fear of untidiness
Bogyphobia	fear of goblins
Brontophobia	fear of thunder
Carcinomaphobia	fear of cancer
Catoptrophobia	fear of mirrors
Chaetophobia	fear of hair
Cheimaphobia	fear of cold
Chorophobia	fear of dancing
Chronophobia	fear of time
Cibophobia	fear of food
Clinophobia	fear of going to bed
Cynophobia	fear of dogs
Demophobia	fear of crowds
Dentophobia	fear of dentists
Ergasiophobia	fear of work
Gamophobia	fear of marriage
Gerascophobia	fear of ageing
Gynaephobia	fear of women
Hemaphobia	fear of blood
Herpetophobia	fear of reptiles
Hormephobia	fear of shock

Hydrophobia	fear of water
Iatrophobia	fear of doctors
Kenophobia	fear of empty rooms
Lachanaphobia	fear of vegetables
Methyphobia	fear of alcohol
Mysophobia	fear of dirt
Necrophobia	fear of death, corpses
Nosocomephobia	fear of hospitals
Oenophobia	fear of wine
Olfactophobia	fear of smells
Ommatophobia	fear of eyes
Ophidiophobia	fear of snakes
Peladophobia	fear of baldness
Pharmacophobia	fear of drugs
Philemaphobia	fear of kissing
Photophobia	fear of light
Pogonophobia	fear of beards
Pyrophobia	fear of fire
Rhytiphobia	fear of getting wrinkles
Sciophobia	fear of shadows
Scopophobia	fear of being looked at
Selenophobia	fear of the moon
Soceraphobia	fear of parents-in-law
Stasiphobia	fear of standing
Taphephobia	fear of being buried alive
Thaasophobia	fear of sitting
Tocophobia	fear of childbirth
Tomophobia	fear of surgery
Trypanophobia	fear of injections
Venustaphobia	fear of beautiful women
Xenophobia	fear of foreigners
Xerophobia	fear of dryness
Zelophobia	fear of jealousy

RHYMING SLANG

Apples and pears	Stairs
Barnet fair	Hair
Currant bun	Sun
Whistle and flute	Suit
Tit for tat	Hat
Trouble and strife	Wife
Skin and blister	Sister
Pen and ink	Stink
Loaf of bread	Head
Plates of meat	Feet
Daisy roots	Boots
Boat race	Face
Saucepan lids	Kids
Rosy Lee	Tea
Half inch	Pinch (to steal)
Dog and bone	'Phone
Adam and Eve	Believe
Bread and honey	Money
Brown bread	Dead
China plate	Mate
Frog and toad	Road
Mince pies	Eyes
Pork pies	Lies
Ruby Murray	Curry
Syrup of fig	Wig
Tom and Dick	Sick
Old Joanna	Piano

COLLECTORS AND ENTHUSIASTS

INTEREST	NAME
Antiquities	Antiquary
Ants	Myrmecologist
Ballet	Balletomane
Banknotes	Notaphilist
Beer mats	Tegestologist
Beetles	Coleopterist

Bell-ringing	Campanologist
Birds	Ornithologist
Bookbinding	Bibliopegist
Books	Bibliophile, bibliomane, bibliolatrist
Butterflies, Moths	Lepidopterist
Cats	Ailurophile
Caves	Speleologist
Coins, Medals	Numismatist
Crossword puzzles	Cruciverbamorist
Diaries, journal-keeping	Ephemerist
Dogs	Canophilist
Dolls	Plangonology
Ferns	Pteridophilist
Flags, Banners	Vexillologist
Food and drink	Gourmet, epicure
Horses	Hippophile

Insects	Entomologist
Keys	Cagophilist
Learning, literature	Philologist
Mankind, the welfare of	Philanthropist
Matchboxes	Cumyxaphilist
Reptiles	Herpetologist
Secret writing, cryptography	Steganographer
Shells	Conchologist
Silkworms	Sericulturist
Snakes	Ophiophilist
Spiders	Arachnologist
Stamps	Philatelist
Teddy bears	Arctophile
UFOs	Ufologist
Wine	Oenophile
Words, correct pronunciation of	Orthoepist

NEW WORDS

A selection of words added to the Oxford English Dictionary in 2006

adhocracy, *n.*; baby blues, *n.*; binge eater, *n.*; chuffing, *v.*; cinephile, *n.*; corporatise, *n.*; cross-party, *adj.*; Eeyorish, *adj.*; fugly, *n.* and *adj.*; hinky, *adj.*; jobseeker, *n.*; ladyboy, *n.*; La Niña, *n.*; self-medicator, *n.*; superminicomputer, *n.*; tag sale, *n.*; Talibanisation, *n.*; thigh-high, *adv.*, *adj.* and *n.*; unelectable, *adj.*; webcaster, *n.*

LINGUISTIC TERMS

WORD	DEFINITION	EXAMPLE
Acronym	Abbreviation formed from the first letters of each word	BBC = British Broadcasting Corporation
Anagram	Word(s) rearranged to produce new word(s)	earth/heart
Antonym	Words with opposite meanings	hot/cold
Archaism	Word or expression from an earlier time that is no longer in use	thou art = you are
Euphemism	Word or phrase used in place of a term considered too direct	pushing up daisies = dead
Homonym	Words with the same pronunciation and spelling but different meanings	mean (average, nasty) tongue (language, organ)
Malapropism	Word or phrase used incorrectly in place of a similar sounding word	Michelangelo painted the Sixteenth Chapel
Neologism	Word invented to describe an existing concept	email
Palindrome	Word or sentence that reads the same in both directions	Do geese see God?
Pangram	Sentence containing all the letters of the alphabet	Pack my box with five dozen liquor jugs
Portmanteau	New word made from a combination of two or more existing words	Oxbridge = Oxford and Cambridge universities
Spoonerism	Accidental transposition of the first letters or parts of words in speech	belly jeans
Synonym	Different words with the same meaning	chair/seat

-ARCHIES AND -OCRACIES

Anarchy	Social or political disorder
Aristocracy	Privileged group, nobility
Autarchy	Absolute sovereignty
Autocracy	Absolute rule by one person
Bureaucracy	Rule by administration, officialdom
Democracy	Rule by the people via elected representatives
Despotocracy	Absolute rule by a tyrant or oppressor
Diarchy	Rule by two independent authorities
Ethnocracy	Rule by an ethnic or racial group
Gerontocracy	Rule by the elderly
Gynarchy, Gynocracy, Gynaecocracy	Rule by women
Hierocracy	A body of ruling priests
Matriarchy	Social organisation where mother is head
Meritocracy	Rule by persons selected according to merit
Monarchy	Rule by monarch
Monocracy	Rule by one person only
Ochlocracy	Mob rule
Oligarchy	Rule by a small group of people
Patriarchy	Rule by a man with descent through the male line
Plutocracy	Rule by the wealthy
Stratocracy	Military rule
Technocracy	Rule by technical experts
Thearchy	Rule by a god or gods
Triarchy	Rule by three people

BOOKS OF THE BIBLE

The following list gives the commonly used abbreviations for the books of the Bible.

OLD TESTAMENT

Genesis	Gen.	Joshua	Josh.
Exodus	Exod.	Judges	Judg.
Leviticus	Lev.	Ruth	Ruth
Numbers	Num.	1 Samuel	1 Sam.
Deuteronomy	Deut.	2 Samuel	2 Sam.
		1 Kings	1 Kgs.
		2 Kings	2 Kgs.
		1 Chronicles	1 Chr.
		2 Chronicles	2 Chr.
		Ezra	Ezra

Nehemiah	Neh.
Esther	Esther
Job	Job
Psalms	Ps.
Proverbs	Prov.
Ecclesiastes	Eccles.
Song of Solomon	S. of S.
Isaiah	Isa.
Jeremiah	Jer.
Lamentations	Lam.
Ezekiel	Ezek.
Daniel	Dan.
Hosea	Hos.
Joel	Joel
Amos	Amos
Obadiah	Obad.
Jonah	Jon.
Micah	Mic.
Nahum	Nah.
Habakkuk	Hab.
Zephaniah	Zeph.
Haggai	Hag.
Zechariah	Zech.
Malachi	Mal.

APOCRYPHA

1 Esdras	1 Esd.
2 Esdras	2 Esd.
Tobit	Tobit
Judith	Judith
Rest of Esther	Rest of Esth.
Wisdom of Solomon	Wisd.
Ecclesiasticus	Ecclus.
Baruch with the Epistle of Jeremy	Baruch and Ep. of Jer.
Song of the Three Holy Children	S. of III Ch.

History of Susanna	Sus.
Bel and the Dragon	Bel & Dr.
Prayer of Manasses	Pr. of Man.
1 Maccabees	1 Macc.
2 Maccabees	2 Macc.

NEW TESTAMENT

Matthew	Matt.
Mark	Mark
Luke	Luke
John	John
Acts	Acts
Romans	Rom.
1 Corinthians	1 Cor.
2 Corinthians	2 Cor.
Galatians	Gal.
Ephesians	Eph.
Philippians	Phil.
Colossians	Col.
1 Thessalonians	1 Thess.
2 Thessalonians	2 Thess.
1 Timothy	1 Tim.
2 Timothy	2 Tim.
Titus	Titus
Philemon	Philem.
Hebrews	Heb.
James	Jas.
1 Peter	1 Pet.
2 Peter	2 Pet.
1 John	1 John
2 John	2 John
3 John	3 John
Jude	Jude
Revelation	Rev.

SINS AND VIRTUES

In 1589, witchhunter Peter Binsfield (c.1545–98) compiled his *Classification of Demons*, in which he paired each of the seven deadly sins with a demon who tempted people by means of the associated sin. The pairings are as follows:

Envy – Leviathan
Gluttony – Beelzebub
Greed – Mammon
Lust – Asmodeus
Pride – Lucifer
Sloth – Belphegor
Wrath – Satan

The Seven Holy Virtues are derived from the epic *Psychomachia*, written by Roman poet Prudentius (c.410), describing their defeat of evil vices. Practising these virtues is alleged to protect against temptation from the Seven Deadly Sins, with each one having its counterpart.

Kindness (Envy)
Abstinence (Gluttony)
Liberality (Greed)
Chastity (Lust)
Humility (Pride)
Diligence (Sloth)
Patience (Wrath)

THE TEN COMMANDMENTS

1. You shall have no other gods but me.
2. You shall not make or worship any idol.
3. You shall not take the name of the Lord in vain.
4. Remember the Sabbath day and keep it holy.
5. Honour your father and mother.
6. You shall not kill.
7. You shall not commit adultery.
8. You shall not steal.
9. You shall not bear false witness.
10. You shall not covet.

Source: Exodus 20:2–17

POPULAR NAMES

Most popular baby names in the UK in 2006 (change from 2005 is in brackets)

BOYS	GIRLS
1. Jack (–)	1. Olivia (+3)
2. Thomas (+1)	2. Grace (+5)
3. Joshua (–1)	3. Jessica (–2)
4. Oliver (+1)	4. Ruby (+11)
5. Harry (+4)	5. Emily (–3)
6. James (–2)	6. Sophie (–2)
7. William (+1)	7. Chloe (–2)
8. Samuel (–1)	8. Lucy (–)
9. Daniel (–3)	9. Lily (+7)
10. Charlie (+2)	10. Ellie (–4)

Most popular baby names in the UK (1904–94)

YEAR	BOYS	GIRLS
1904	William	Mary
1914	John	Mary
1924	John	Margaret
1934	John	Margaret
1944	John	Margaret
1954	David	Susan

1964	David	Susan
1974	Paul	Sarah
1984	Christopher	Sarah
1994	Thomas	Rebecca

AMERICANISMS

Aluminium	aluminum
Autumn	fall
Biscuit	cookie
Braces	suspenders
Bum-bag	fanny pack
Candy floss	cotton candy
Car bonnet	hood
Car park	parking lot
Caretaker	janitor
Cashier	teller
Chemist's	drugstore
Chimney	smokestack
Condom	rubber
Courgette	zucchini
Current account	checking account
Curtains	drapes
Dinner jacket	tuxedo
Drainpipe	downspout
Drawing pin	thumb tack
Estate agent	realtor
Flick knife	switchblade
Ice lolly	popsicle
Jam	jelly
Jug	pitcher
Nappy	diaper
Ladybird	ladybug
Lorry	truck
Noughts & crosses	tic tac toe
Okra	gumbo
Pavement	sidewalk
Petrol	gas
Post code	zip code
Pushchair	stroller
Quilt	comforter
Rubbish	garbage, trash
Sideboards	sideburns
Skipping rope	jumping rope
Spanner	wrench
String	cord
Suitcase	valise
Sweets	candy
Tallboy	highboy
Tap	faucet
Telephone box	phone booth
Torch	flashlight
Tram	streetcar
Trousers	pants
Windscreen	windshield
Zed	zee

THE TWELVE DAYS OF CHRISTMAS

A partridge in a pear tree
Two turtle doves
Three French hens
Four calling birds
Five gold rings
Six geese a-laying
Seven swans a-swimming
Eight maids a-milking
Nine ladies dancing
Ten lords a-leaping
Eleven pipers piping
Twelve drummers drumming

CHRISTMAS CAROLS

The most popular Christmas carols according to a Classic FM poll; date in brackets indicates the year of composition.

1. 'O Holy Night' (1847)
2. 'Silent Night' (1816)
3. 'Hark the Herald Angels Sing' (1840)
4. 'In the Bleak Midwinter' (Holst) (1906)
5. 'In the Bleak Midwinter' (Darke) (1911)
6. 'O Little Town of Bethlehem' (1868)
7. 'Once in Royal David's City' (1849)
8. 'Shepherds' Farewell' (1853)
9. 'O Come, All Ye Faithful' (c.1743)
10. 'It Came Upon the Midnight Clear' (1850)

MATHEMATICS

NUMBERS

Binary numbers: the binary system, or binary notation, uses only the binary digits 0 and 1 to represent any number. The more usual decimal system, using all 10 digits from 0 to 9, has a base of 10; the binary system has a base of 2. Binary notation is the number system most commonly used in computers since the two numerals correspond to the on and off positions of an electronic switch.

Binary numbers from 1 to 20 with their decimal equivalents:

1	1	11	1011
2	10	12	1100
3	11	13	1101
4	100	14	1110
5	101	15	1111
6	110	16	10000
7	111	17	10001
8	1000	18	10010
9	1001	19	10011
10	1010	20	10100

To decipher binary numbers, remember the following rules:
• ignore all noughts in the calculation
• count the right column as 1
• count the second column on the right as 2
• count the third column on the right as 4
• count the fourth column on the right as 8
• count the fifth column on the right as 16, and so on

Cube root: see Cubic number.

Cubic number: the product of multiplying a whole number by itself, and then the product of that by the whole number again, e.g. $3 \times 3 \times 3 = 27$. Therefore 3 is the cube root of 27.

Difference: the result when one number is subtracted from another.

Even number: a whole number that divides by 2 exactly, e.g. to give a whole number without leaving a remainder.

Factor: a whole number that divides into another number without leaving a remainder.

Fibonacci numbers (Leonardo Fibonacci, c.1170–c.1250): beginning 1, 1, a series of numbers in which each number is the sum of the two numbers preceding it, e.g. 1, 1, 2 (1 + 1), 3 (1 + 2), 5 (2 + 3), 8 (3 + 5), 13, 21, 34, 55, etc. This sequence appears in nature, e.g. as the number of petals on the rim of a sunflower, the pattern of scales on a pine cone and the spiral shape of a nautilus shell.

Highest common factor (HCF): the largest number that divides into two or more numbers without leaving a remainder is the HCF of the numbers.

Index: a number placed above the line after another number to show how many times the number on the line is to be multiplied by itself (e.g. 42). The value of the index is called the power.

Integer: any positive or negative whole number, including zero.

Irrational number: a number that cannot be expressed as a fraction or ratio of integers.

Lowest common multiple (LCM): the smallest number that divides by two or more numbers without leaving a remainder is the LCM of the numbers.

Modulus (of a number): its magnitude, ignoring sign, e.g. the modulus of both 3 and -3 is 3.

Multiple: a number that is the product of a given number and any other integer.

Natural (or whole) number: a number that is a positive integer.

Odd number: an integer that will not divide by 2 without leaving a remainder.

Perfect number: a number that is equal to the sum of its factors, excluding the number itself. Only 30 have been discovered so far, the first of which is 6: factors of 6 (excluding 6 itself) are
1, 2 and 3
1 + 2 + 3 = 6

Prime number: with the exception of 1, any natural number that can only be divided by itself and 1.

Prime numbers between 1 and 1000

2	3	5	7	11	13	17
19	23	29	31	37	41	43
47	53	59	61	67	71	73
79	83	89	97	101	103	107
109	113	127	131	137	139	149
151	157	163	167	173	179	181
191	193	197	199	211	223	227
229	233	239	241	251	257	263
269	271	277	281	283	293	307
311	313	317	331	337	347	349
353	359	367	373	379	383	389
397	401	409	419	421	431	433
439	443	449	457	461	463	467
479	487	491	499	503	509	521
523	541	547	557	563	569	571
577	587	593	599	601	607	613
617	619	631	641	643	647	653
659	661	673	677	683	691	701
709	719	727	733	739	743	751

757	761	769	773	787	797	809
811	821	823	827	829	839	853
857	859	863	877	881	883	887
907	911	919	929	937	941	947
953	967	971	977	983	991	997

Product: the result of multiplying numbers together.

Quotient: the result of dividing one number by another number. Also referred to as a ratio.

Ratio: see Quotient.

Rational number: any number that can be expressed as a quotient of integers.

Remainder: the amount left over when one number cannot be exactly divided by another.

Square number: the product of multiplying a whole number by itself, e.g. 3 x 3 = 9. Therefore, 3 is the square root of 9.

Whole number: see Natural number

Unity: the number 1

FRACTIONS, DECIMALS AND PERCENTAGES

Fraction: any quantity expressed as a ratio of two numbers, a numerator and a denominator (see below), written one above the other, separated by a line. When the numerator is less than the denominator, the fraction is of magnitude less than unity.

Decimal point: a dot that separates whole numbers from the fractional part in a decimal notation number.

Decimal fraction: a quantity less than unity expressed in decimal notation, e.g. 0.375.

Denominator: the number below the line in a fraction that denotes the number of equal parts into which the numerator is divided.

Improper fraction: a fraction in which the numerator is larger than the denominator, e.g. $^{13}/_{12}$.

Mixed number: a number that comprises an integer and a fraction, e.g. $4\frac{1}{2}$ (in other words 4 + $\frac{1}{2}$).

Numerator: the number above the line in a fraction which denotes the number of fractional parts taken.

Proper fraction: one in which the numerator is smaller than the denominator, e.g. $^{7}/_{12}$.

Recurring (fractions, decimals and percentages): a pattern that repeats indefinitely.

Vulgar fraction (also known as simple and common fraction): a quantity expressed as a fraction with integers as numerator and denominator, as opposed to being expressed as a decimal fraction, e.g. ¼ rather than 0.25.

CORRESPONDING FRACTIONS, DECIMALS AND PERCENTAGES

These are three different ways of showing the same information:

FRACTION	DECIMAL	PER CENT (%)
¹/₂₀	0.05	5.00
¹/₁₀	0.10	10.00
¹/₉	0.11111*	11.11
¹/₈	0.125	12.50
¹/₇	0.14286	14.28
¹/₆	0.16667*	16.67
¹/₅	0.20	20.00
¼	0.25	25.00
¹/₃	0.33333*	33.33
½	0.50	50.00
²/₃	0.66667*	66.66
¾	0.75	75.00

* = recurring; by convention a recurring digit equal to or greater than 5 is rounded up

GEOMETRY AND TRIGONOMETRY

Geometry is the branch of mathematics that deals with the properties of lines, points, surfaces and solids.

Acute angle: an angle of less than 90°, e.g. less than a quarter of a complete rotation.

Cosine of an angle (abbrev. cos): in a right-angled triangle, the ratio of the side adjacent to the given angle to the hypotenuse.

Degree (°): the magnitude of an angle of ¹/₃₆₀ of a complete rotation.

Hypotenuse: the side of a right-angled triangle that is opposite the right angle.

Right angle: a quarter of a complete rotation in angle (90°).

Sine of an angle (abbrev. sin): in a right-angled triangle, the ratio of the side opposite the given angle to the hypotenuse.

Tangent of an angle (abbrev. tan): in a right-angled triangle, the ratio of the side opposite the given angle to the adjacent side.

Trigonometry: the branch of mathematics that deals with the relations between the sides and angles of triangles.

POLYGONS

A polygon is a closed plane figure with three or more straight sides (usually implies more than four).

NUMBER OF SIDES	NAME OF POLYGON
3	triangle
4	quadrilateral
5	pentagon
6	hexagon
7	heptagon
8	octagon
9	nonagon
10	decagon
12	dodecagon

Equilateral triangle: a triangle which has three equal sides; each of its internal angles is 60°.

Isosceles triangle: a triangle in which two of the sides are of equal length.

Parallelogram: a quadrilateral whose opposite sides are parallel and equal in length.

Pythagoras' theorem (Greek mathematician and philosopher, c.580–c.500 BC): the square drawn on the hypotenuse is equal in size to the sum of the squares drawn on the other two sides.

Rectangle: a rhombus whose vertices are all at right angles.

Rhombus: a parallelogram whose sides are of equal length.

Scalene triangle: a triangle with unequal length sides and no axes of symmetry.

Square: a rectangle with equal length sides.

Trapezium: a quadrilateral with two parallel sides of unequal length.

Vertex (plural vertices): the point at which two sides of a polygon meet.

CIRCLES AND OTHER CONIC SECTIONS

Circle: a plane figure bounded by one line, every point on which is an equal distance from a fixed point at the centre.

Arc: any part of the circumference of a circle.

Circumference: the line that forms the complete perimeter of a circle.

Diameter: a straight line that passes through the centre of a circle (or other figure) and terminates at the circumference at each end.

pi (indicated by the Greek letter π): the ratio of the circumference of a circle to its diameter (approximately 3.141592...).

Radius (plural radii): a straight line from the circumference of a circle to its centre.

ANGULAR AND CIRCULAR MEASURES

60 seconds ($''$) = 1 minute ($'$)

60 minutes = 1 degree (°)

90 degrees = 1 right angle or quadrant

Circumference of circle = diameter (or 2 x radius) x 3.1416, e.g. πd or $2\pi r$

Area of circle = radius squared x 3.1416, e.g. πr^2

Surface of sphere = 4 x radius squared x 3.1416, e.g. $4\pi r^2$

Volume of sphere = ⅘ x radius cubed x 0.523, e.g. ⅘ πr^3

Radius* = one degree of circumference x 57.3, e.g. $360/2\pi$

Curved surface of cylinder = circumference of circular base x 3.1416 x length or height, e.g. $2\pi rh$

Volume of cylinder = area of circular base x length or height, e.g. $\pi r^2 h$

*Or, one radian (the angle subtended at the centre of a circle by an arc of the circumference equal in length to the radius) = 57.3 degrees

π TO 100 DECIMAL PLACES

3.14159265358979323846264338327
9502884197169399375105820974
944592307816406286208998628034
8253421170679

MATHEMATICAL SYMBOLS

$=$	Equal to
$\neq$	Not equal to
$\approx$	Approximately equal to
$\equiv$	Identically equal to
$\div$	Divide
x	Multiplication
∞	Infinity
$\propto$	Proportional to
$\parallel$	Parallel to
$\perp$	Perpendicular to
$\geq$	Greater than or equal to
$\ngeq$	Not greater than or equal to
$>$	Greater than
$\ngtr$	Not greater than
$\gg$	Much greater than
$\gtrless$	Greater than or less than
$\leq$	Less than or equal to
$\nleq$	Not less than or equal to
$<$	Less than
$\nless$	Not less than
$\ll$	Much less than
$\lessgtr$	Less than or greater than
$\pm$	Plus or minus
$\int$	Integral sign
$\sqrt{\ }$	Square root
$\sqrt[3]{\ }$	Cube root
$\sqrt[n]{\ }$	n-th root
∂	Partial differentiation
Σ	Sum of

ROMAN NUMERALS

1	I	30	XXX
2	II	40	XL
3	III	50	L
4	IV	60	LX
5	V	70	LXX
6	VI	80	LXXX
7	VII	90	XC
8	VIII	100	C
9	IX	200	CC
10	X	300	CCC
11	XI	400	CD
12	XII	500	D
13	XIII	600	DC
14	XIV	700	DCC
15	XV	800	DCCC
16	XVI	900	CM
17	XVII	1000	M
18	XVIII	1500	MD
19	XIX	1900	MCM
20	XX	2000	MM

EXAMPLES

43	XLIII
66	LXVI
98	XCVIII
339	CCCXXXIX
619	DCXIX
988	CMLXXXVIII
996	CMXCVI
1674	MDCLXXIV
1962	MCMLXII
1998	MCMXCVIII
2008	MMVIII

A bar placed over a numeral has the effect of multiplying the number by 1,000, e.g.

6,000	$\overline{\text{VI}}$
16,000	$\overline{\text{XVI}}$
160,000	$\overline{\text{CLX}}$
666,000	$\overline{\text{DCLXVI}}$

PROBABILITY AND STATISTICS

Probability is a branch of mathematics concerned with chance. It usually begins with a collection of data which is then analysed to identify trends and predict likely outcomes.

MEAN
The mean is found by dividing the sum of quantities by the number of quantities. It is often referred to as 'average'.

MODE
In almost any set of figures, the number which occurs most often is called the mode.

MEDIAN
The median is the middle number in a set of numbers arranged in order of size. If there are two middle numbers then the median is the average of the two figures.

GAUSSIAN CURVES
A line graph or bar chart showing the distribution of data around an average value will produce a distinctive-looking curve. In other words the Gaussian curve is obtained by plotting random variation around the mean.

BINARY COMPUTER CODING

The binary system is a way of counting using just the two numbers 0 and 1. Morse code is an early example of a binary code, using dots and dashes instead of 0s and 1s. Computer programs are translated into binary code before they can be used.

0	00000000
1	00000001
2	00000010
9	00001001
10	00001010
11	00001011
12	00001100
13	00001101
14	00001110
15	00001111
16	00010000
17	00010001
18	00010010
32	00100000
33	00100001
64	01000000
65	01000001
119	01110111
120	01111000
121	01111001
122	01111010
123	01111011

MONEY

WORLD CURRENCIES

Average rate against £1 Sterling on 30 March 2007

COUNTRY/TERRITORY	CURRENCY	VALUE
Afghanistan	Afghani (Af) of 100 puls	Af 77.75
Albania	Lek (Lk) of 100 qindraka	Lk 186.44
Algeria	Algerian dinar (DA) of 100 centimes	DA 141.38
American Samoa	Currency is that of the USA	US$1.98
Andorra	Euro (€) of 100 cents	€1.47
Angola	Readjusted kwanza (Krzl) of 100 lwei	Kzrl 158.16
Anguilla	East Caribbean dollar (EC$) of 100 cents	EC$5.34
Antigua and Barbuda	East Caribbean dollar (EC$) of 100 cents	EC$5.34
Argentina	Peso of 10,000 australes	Pesos 6.13
Armenia	Dram of 100 louma	Dram 714.12
Aruba	Aruban guilder	Guilder 3.54
Ascension Island	Currency is that of St Helena	
Australia	Australian dollar ($A) of 100 cents	$A2.42
Austria	Euro (€) of 100 cents	€1.47
Azerbaijan	New manat of 100 gopik	New manat 1.71
The Bahamas	Bahamian dollar (B$) of 100 cents	B$1.98
Bahrain	Bahraini dinar (BD) of 1,000 fils	BD 0.73
Bangladesh	Taka (Tk) of 100 poisha	Tk 134.99
Barbados	Barbados dollar (BD$) of 100 cents	BD$3.92
Belarus	Belarusian rouble of 100 kopeks	BYR 4,206.12
Belgium	Euro (€) of 100 cents	€1.47
Belize	Belize dollar (BZ$) of 100 cents	BZ$3.86
Benin	Franc CFA	Francs 970.07
Bermuda	Bermuda dollar of 100 cents	$1.96
Bhutan	Ngultrum of 100 chetrum (Indian currency is also legal tender)	Ngultrum 85.97
Bolivia	Boliviano ($b) of 100 centavos	$b15.681
Bosnia and Hercegovina	Convertible marka	Marka 2.88
Botswana	Pula (P) of 100 thebe	P 12.26
Brazil	Real of 100 centavos	Real 4.01
Brunei	Brunei dollar (B$) of 100 sen	B$2.98
Bulgaria	Lev of 100 stotinki	Leva 2.89

COUNTRY/TERRITORY	CURRENCY	VALUE
Burkina Faso	Franc CFA	Francs 970.07
Burundi	Burundi franc of 100 centimes	Francs 2,042.95
Cambodia	Riel of 100 sen	Riel 7,875.23
Cameroon	Franc CFA	Francs 970.07
Canada	Canadian dollar (C$) 100 cents	C$2.26
Cape Verde	Escudo Caboverdiano of 100 centavos	Esc 162.96
Cayman Islands	Cayman Islands dollar (CI$) of 100 cents	CI$1.70
Central African Republic	Franc CFA	Francs 970.07
Chad	Franc CFA	Francs 970.07
Chile	Chilean peso of 100 centavos	Pesos 1,056.87
China	Renminbi Yuan of 10 jiao or 100 fen	Yuan 15.16
Colombia	Colombian peso of 100 centavos	Pesos 4,320.71
The Comoros	Comorian franc (KMF) of 100 centimes	Francs 727.55
Congo, Rep. of	Franc CFA	Francs 970.07
Congo, Dem. Rep. of	Congolese franc	CFr 1,112.09
Cook Islands	Currency is that of New Zealand	NZ$2.74
Costa Rica	Costa Rican colón (C) of 100 céntimos	C1,017.59
Côte d'Ivoire	Franc CFA	Francs 970.07
Croatia	Kuna of 100 lipa	Kuna 10.99
Cuba	Cuban peso of 100 centavos	Pesos 1.96
Cyprus	Cyprus pound (C£) of 100 cents	C£0.86
Czech Republic	Koruna (Kcs) of 100 haléru	Kcs 41.29
Denmark	Danish krone of 100 øre	Kroner 10.98
Djibouti	Djibouti franc of 100 centimes	Francs 347.22
Dominica	East Caribbean dollar (EC$) of 100 cents	EC$5.34
Dominican Republic	Dominican Republic peso(RD$) of 100 centavos	RD$63.94
East Timor	Currency is that of the USA	US$1.98
Ecuador	Currency is that of the USA (formerly sucre of 100 centavos)	US$1.98
Egypt	Egyptian pound (£E) of 100 piastres or 1,000 millièmes	£E11.17
El Salvador	Currency is that of USA	US$1.98
Equatorial Guinea	Franc CFA	Francs 970.07
Eritrea	Nakfa	Nakfa 29.63
Estonia	Kroon of 100 sents	Kroons 23.05
Ethiopia	Ethiopian birr (EB) of 100 cents	EB 17.43
Faeroe Islands	Currency is that of Denmark	Kroner 10.98

COUNTRY/TERRITORY	CURRENCY	VALUE
Falkland Islands	Falkland pound of 100 pence	
Fiji	Fiji dollar (F$) of 100 cents	F$3.23
Finland	Euro (€) of 100 cents	€1.47
France	Euro (€) of 100 cents	€1.47
French Guiana	Euro (€) of 100 cents	€1.47
French Polynesia	Franc CFP	Francs 175.71
Gabon	Franc CFA	Francs 970.07
Gambia	Dalasi (D) of 100 butut	D 53.74
Georgia	Laria of 100 tetri	Laria 3.33
Germany	Euro (€) of 100 cents	€1.47
Ghana	Cedi of 100 pesewas	Cedi 18,191.53
Gibraltar	Gibraltar pound of 100 pence	
Greece	Euro (€) of 100 cents	€1.47
Greenland	Currency is that of Denmark	Kroner 10.98
Grenada	East Caribbean dollar (EC$) of 100 cents	EC$5.34
Guadeloupe	Euro (€) of 100 cents	€1.47
Guam	Currency is that of the USA	US$1.98
Guatemala	Quetzal (Q) of 100 centavos	Q 15.10
Guinea	Guinea franc of 100 centimes	Francs 11,768.11
Guinea-Bissau	Franc CFA	Francs 970.07
Guyana	Guyana dollar (G$) of 100 cents	G$397.97
Haiti	Gourde of 100 centimes	Gourdes 71.88
Honduras	Lempira of 100 centavos	Lempiras 37.05
Hong Kong	Hong Kong (HK$) of 100 cents	HK$15.32
Hungary	Forint of 100 fillér	Forints 364.43
Iceland	Icelandic króna (Kr) of 100 aurar	Kr 129.50
India	Indian rupee (Rs) of 100 paisa	Rs 85.25
Indonesia	Rupiah (Rp) of 100 sen	Rp 17,897.32
Iran	Rial	Rials 18,132.68
Iraq	New Iraqi dinar (NID)	NID 2,510.77
Ireland, Republic of	Euro (€) of 100 cents	€1.47
Israel	Shekel of 100 agora	Shekels 8.15
Italy	Euro (€) of 100 cents	€1.47
Jamaica	Jamaican dollar (J$) of 100 cents	J$132.83
Japan	Yen	Yen 231.59
Jordan	Jordanian dinar (JD) of 1,000 fils	JD 1.39
Kazakhstan	Tenge	Tenge 242.83
Kenya	Kenya shilling (Ksh) of 100 cents	Ksh 134.65

COUNTRY/TERRITORY	CURRENCY	VALUE
Kiribati	Australian dollar ($A) of 100 cents	$A2.42
Korea, Dem. People's Rep. Of	Won of 100 chon	Won 335.85
Korea, Republic of	Won	Won 1,844.85
Kuwait	Kuwaiti dinar (KD) of 1,000 fils	KD 0.57
Kyrgyzstan	Som	Som 74.65
Laos	Kip (K) of 100 at	K 19,044.55
Latvia	Lats of 100 santims	Lats 1.05
Lebanon	Lebanese pound (L£) of of 100 piastres	L£2,965.56
Lesotho	Loti (M) of 100 lisente	M 14.22
Liberia	Liberian dollar (L$) of 100 cents	L$119.53
Libya	Libyan dinar (LD) of 1,000 dirhams	LD 2.52
Liechtenstein	Swiss franc of 100 rappen (or centimes)	Francs 2.40
Lithuania	Litas of 100 centas	Litas 5.09
Luxembourg	Euro (€) of 100 cents	€1.47
Macao	Pataca of 100 avos	Pataca 15.78
Macedonia	Denar of 100 deni	Den 90.08
Madagascar	Ariary of 5 iraimbilanja	MGA 3,830.71
Malawi	Kwacha (K) of 100 tambala	MK 273.94
Malaysia	Malaysian dollar (ringgit) (M$) of 100 sen	M$6.78
Maldives	Rufiyaa of 100 laaris	Rufiyaa 25.32
Mali	Franc CFA	Francs 970.07
Malta	Maltese lira (LM) of 100 cents of 1,000 mils	LM 0.63
Marshall Islands	Currency is that of the USA	US$1.98
Martinique	Currency is that of France	€1.47
Mauritania	Ouguiya (UM) of 5 khoums	UM 531.91
Mauritius	Mauritius rupee of 100 cents	Rs 63.16
Mayotte	Currency is that of France	€1.47
Mexico	Peso of 100 centavos	Pesos 21.59
Micronesia	Currency is that of the USA	US$1.98
Moldova	Moldovan leu of 100 bani	MDL 24.55
Monaco	Euro (€) of 100 cents	€1.47
Mongolia	Tugrik of 100 möngö	Tugriks 2,284.97
Montenegro	Euro (€) of 100 cents	€1.47
Montserrat	East Caribbean dollar (EC$) of 100 cents	EC$5.34
Morocco	Dirham (DH) of 100 centimes	DH 16.45
Mozambique	New Metical (MT) of 100 centavos (?)	MT 51.94

COUNTRY/TERRITORY	CURRENCY	VALUE
Myanmar	Kyat (K) of 100 pyas	K 12.68
Namibia	Namibian dollar of 100 cents	
Nauru	Australian dollar ($A) of 100 cents	$A2.42
Nepal	Nepalese rupee of 100 paisa	Rs 136.40
The Netherlands	Euro (€) of 100 cents	€1.47
Netherlands Antilles	Netherlands Antilles guilder of 100 cents	Guilders 3.54
New Caledonia	Franc CFP	Francs 175.71
New Zealand	New Zealand dollar (NZ$) of 100 cents	NZ$2.74
Nicaragua	Córdoba (C$) of 100 centavos	C$35.73
Niger	Franc CFA	Francs 970.07
Nigeria	Naira (N) of 100 kobo	N 250.95
Niue	Currency is that of New Zealand	NZ$2.74
Norfolk Island	Currency is that of Australia	$A2.42
Northern Mariana Islands	Currency is that of the USA	US$1.98
Norway	Krone of 100 øre	Kroner 11.97
Oman	Rial Omani (OR) of 1,000 baisas	OR 0.75
Pakistan	Pakistan rupee of 100 paisa	Rs 119.14
Palau	Currency is that of the USA	US$1.98
Panama	Balboa of 100 centésimos (US notes are in circulation)	Balboa 1.96
Papua New Guinea	Kina (K) of 100 toea	K 5.83
Paraguay	Guarani (Gs) of 100 céntimos	Gs 9,963.67
Peru	New Sol of 100 cénts	New Sol 6.24
The Philippines	Philippine peso (P) of 100 centavos	P 94.64
Pitcairn Islands	Currency is that of New Zealand	NZ$2.74
Poland	Zloty of 100 groszy	Zlotych 5.68
Portugal	Euro (€) of 100 cents	€1.47
Puerto Rico	Currency is that of the USA	US$1.98
Qatar	Qatar riyal of 100 dirhams	Riyals 7.14
Réunion	Currency is that of France	€1.47
Romania	New leu of 100 bani	Lei 4.94
Russian Federation	Rouble of 100 kopeks	Rbl 51.06
Rwanda	Rwanda franc of 100 centimes	Francs 1,071.78
St Christopher and Nevis	East Caribbean dollar (EC$) of 100 cents	EC$5.34
St Helena	St Helena pound (£) of 100 pence	
St Lucia	East Caribbean dollar (EC$) of 100 cents	EC$5.34

COUNTRY/TERRITORY	CURRENCY	VALUE
St Pierre and Miquelon	Currency is that of France	€1.47
St Vincent and the Grenadines	East Caribbean dollar (EC$) of 100 cents	EC$5.34
Samoa	Tala (S$) of 100 sene	S$5.17
San Marino	Euro (€) of 100 cents	€1.47
São Tomé and Princípe	Dobra of 100 centavos	Dobra 13,368.98
Saudi Arabia	Saudi riyal (SR) of 20 qursh or 100 halala	SR 7.36
Senegal	Franc CFA	Francs 970.07
Serbia	New dinar of 100 paras	New dinars 118.89
Seychelles	Seychelles rupee of 100 cents	Rs 12.01
Sierra Leone	Leone (Le) of 100 cents	Le 5,875.92
Singapore	Singapore dollar (S$) of 100 cents	S$2.98
Slovakia	Koruna (Sk) of 100 halierov	Kcs 48.92
Slovenia	Euro (€) of 100 cents	€1.47
Solomon Islands	Solomon Islands dollar (SI$) of 100 cents	SI$14.97
Somalia	Somali shilling of 100 cents	Shillings 2,680.92
South Africa	Rand (R) of 100 cents	R 14.40
Spain	Euro (€) of 100 cents	€1.47
Sri Lanka	Sri Lankan rupee of 100 cents	Rs 215.59
Sudan	Sudanese pound of 100 piastres	SDG 3.96
Suriname	Surinam dollar of 100 cents	Dollar 5.38
Swaziland	Lilangeni (E) of 100 cents (South African currency is also in circulation)	
Sweden	Swedish krona of 100 öre	Kronor 13.76
Switzerland	Swiss franc of 100 rappen (or centimes)	Francs 2.40
Syria	Syrian pound (S£) of 100 piastres	S£103.15
Taiwan	New Taiwan dollar (NT$) of 100 cents	NT$65.45
Tajikistan	Somoni (TJS) of 100 dirams	—
Tanzania	Tanzanian shilling of 100 cents	Shillings 2,430.11
Thailand	Baht of 100 satang	Baht 68.67
Togo	Franc CFA	Francs 970.07
Tokelau	Currency is that of New Zealand	NZ$2.74
Tonga	Pa'anga (T$) of 100 seniti	T$3.90
Trinidad and Tobago	Trinidad and Tobago dollar (TT$) of 100 cents	TT$12.42
Tristan da Cunha	Currency is that of the UK	—

COUNTRY/TERRITORY	CURRENCY	VALUE
Tunisia	Tunisian dinar of 1,000 millimes	Dinars 2.56
Turkey	New Turkish lira (TL) of 100 kurus	TL 2.75
Turkmenistan	Manat of 100 tenge	Manat 10,273.85
Turks and Caicos Islands	US dollar (US$) of 100 cents	US$1.98
Tuvalu	Australian dollar ($A) of 100 cents	$A2.42
Uganda	Uganda shilling of 100 cents	Shillings 3,431.38
Ukraine	Hryvna of 100 kopiykas	UAH 9.87
United Arab Emirates	UAE dirham (Dh) of 100 fils	Dirham 7.26
United States of America	US dollar (US$) of 100 cents	US$1.98
Uruguay	Uruguayan peso of 100 centésimos	Pesos 47.36
Uzbekistan	Sum of 100 tiyin	Sum 2,451.83
Vanuatu	Vatu of 100 centimes	Vatu 210.94
Vatican City State	Euro (€) of 100 cents	€1.47
Venezuela	Bolívar (Bs) of 100 céntimos	Bs 6,273.14
Vietnam	Dong of 10 hao or 100 xu	Dong 31,420.83
Virgin Islands, British	US dollar (US$) (£ sterling and EC$ also circulate)	US$1.98
Virgin Islands, US	Currency is that of the USA	US$1.98
Wallis and Futuna Islands	Franc CFP	Francs 175.71
Yemen	Riyal of 100 fils	Riyals 389.83
Zambia	Kwacha (K) of 100 ngwee	K 8,296.52
Zimbabwe	Zimbabwe dollar (Z$) of 100 cents	Z$490.34

Franc CFA= Franc se la Communauté financière africaine

Franc CFP = Franc des Comptoirs français du Pacifique

Source: WM/Reuters Closing Spot Rates

BRITISH CURRENCY

The decimal system was introduced on 15 February 1971. The unit of currency is the pound sterling (£) of 100 pence.

COINS

The coins in circulation are:

DENOMINATION	METAL
Penny	bronze
Penny	copper-plated steel
2 pence	bronze
2 pence	copper-plated steel
5 pence	cupro-nickel
10 pence	cupro-nickel
20 pence	cupro-nickel
50 pence	cupro-nickel
£1	nickel-brass
£2	cupro-nickel, nickel-brass

Bronze is an alloy of copper 97 parts, zinc 2.5 parts and tin 0.5 part. These proportions have been subject to slight variations in the past. Bronze was replaced by copper-plated steel in 1992. Cupro-nickel is an alloy of copper 75 parts and nickel 25 parts, except for the 20p, composed of copper 84 parts, nickel 16 parts.

BANKNOTES

Bank of England notes are currently issued in denominations of £5, £10, £20 and £50.

The current series of notes portrays on the back the following prominent figures from British history:

£5	Elizabeth Fry
£10	Charles Darwin
£20	Adam Smith*
£50	Sir John Houblon

* The £20 banknote bearing a portrait of Sir Edward Elgar remains legal tender.

LEGAL TENDER

Gold (dated 1838 onwards, if not below least current weight)	to any amount
£5 (Crown since 1990)	to any amount
£	to any amount
£1	to any amount
50p	up to £10
25p (Crown pre-1990)	up to £10
20p	up to £10
10p	up to £5
5p	up to £5
2p	up to 20p
1p	up to 20p

WITHDRAWN COINS

These coins ceased to be legal tender on the following dates:

Farthing	1960
Halfpenny (½d.)	1969
Half-Crown	1970
Threepence	1971
Penny (1d.)	1971
Sixpence (6d.)	1980
Halfpenny (½p)	1984
old 5 pence	1990
old 10 pence	1993
old 50 pence	1998

The £1 coin was introduced in 1983 to replace the £1 note; no £1 notes have been issued since 1984 and the outstanding £1 notes were written off in March 1998. The 10 shilling note was replaced by the 50p coin in 1969, and ceased to be legal tender in 1970.

SLANG TERMS FOR MONEY

A bob	1 shilling
A quid	£1
A fiver	£5
A tenner	£10
A score	£20
A pony	£25
A monkey	£500
A plum	£100,000
A kite	an accommodation bill

Blunt	silver, or money in general
Browns	copper or bronze
Coppers	copper/bronze small denomination coins
Tin, brass	money generally

THE TRIAL OF THE PYX

The Trial of the Pyx is the examination by a jury to ascertain that coins made by the Royal Mint, which have been set aside in the pyx (or box), are of the proper weight, diameter and composition required by law. The trial is held annually, presided over by the Queen's Remembrancer (the Senior Master of the Supreme Court), with a jury of freemen of the Company of Goldsmiths.

PEOPLE

PRESIDENTS OF THE USA

YEAR INAUGURATED

1789	George Washington (1732–99)	*Federation*
1797	John Adams (1735–1826)	*Federation*
1801	Thomas Jefferson (1743–1826)	*Republican*
1809	James Madison (1751–1836)	*Republican*
1817	James Monroe (1758–1831)	*Republican*
1825	John Quincy Adams (1767–1848)	*Republican*
1829	Andrew Jackson (1767–1845)	*Democrat*
1837	Martin Van Buren (1782–1862)	*Democrat*
1841	William Harrison (1773–1841) (died in office)	*Whig*
1841	John Tyler (1790–1862) (elected as Vice-President)	*Whig*
1845	James Polk (1795–1849)	*Democrat*
1849	Zachary Taylor (1784–1850) (died in office)	*Whig*
1850	Millard Fillmore (1800–74) (elected as Vice-President)	*Whig*
1853	Franklin Pierce (1804–69),	*Democrat*
1857	James Buchanan (1791–1868)	*Democrat*
1861	Abraham Lincoln (1809–65) (assassinated in office)	*Republican*
1865	Andrew Johnson (1808–75) (elected as Vice-President)	*Republican*
1869	Ulysses Grant (1822–85)	*Republican*
1877	Rutherford Hayes (1822–93)	*Republican*
1881	James Garfield (1831–81) (assassinated in office)	*Republican*
1881	Chester Arthur (1830–86) (elected as Vice-President)	*Republican*
1885	Grover Cleveland (1837–1908)	*Democrat*
1889	Benjamin Harrison (1833–1901)	*Republican*
1893	Grover Cleveland (1837–1908)	*Democrat*
1897	William McKinley (1843–1901) (assassinated in office)	*Republican*
1901	Theodore Roosevelt (1858–1919) (elected as Vice-President)	*Republican*
1909	William Taft (1857–1930)	*Republican*

YEAR INAUGURATED

1913	Woodrow Wilson (1856–1924)	*Democrat*
1921	Warren Harding (1865–1923)	
	(died in office)	*Republican*
1923	Calvin Coolidge (1872–1933)	
	(elected as Vice-President)	*Republican*
1929	Herbert Hoover (1874–1964)	*Republican*
1933*	Franklin Roosevelt (1882–1945)	
	(died in office)	*Democrat*
1945	Harry Truman (1884–1972)	
	(elected as Vice-President)	*Democrat*
1953	Dwight Eisenhower (1890–1969)	*Republican*
1961	John Kennedy (1917–63)	
	(assassinated in office)	*Democrat*
1963	Lyndon Johnson (1908–73)	
	(elected as Vice-President)	*Democrat*
1969	Richard Nixon (1913–94)	*Republican*
1974†	Gerald Ford (1913–)	*Republican*
1977	James Carter (1924–)	*Democrat*
1981	Ronald Reagan (1911–2004)	*Republican*
1989	George Bush (1924–)	*Republican*
1993	William Clinton (1946–)	*Democrat*
2000	George W. Bush (1946–)	*Republican*

* Re-elected 5 November 1940, the first case of a third term; re-elected for a fourth term 7 November 1944

† Appointed under the provisions of the 25th Amendment

SECRETARIES-GENERAL OF THE UNITED NATIONS

1946–53	Trygve Lie (Norway)
1953–61	Dag Hammarskjöld (Sweden)
1961–71	U Thant (Burma)
1971–81	Kurt Waldheim (Austria)
1981–91	Javier Pérez de Cuéllar (Peru)
1991–96	Boutros Boutros-Ghali (Egypt)
1996–2007	Kofi Annan (Ghana)
2007	Ban Ki-moon (Republic of Korea)

PRESIDENTS OF THE EUROPEAN PARLIAMENT

1952–54	Henri Spaak (Belgium)	1979–82	Simone Veil (France)
1954	Alcide de Gasperi (Italy)	1982–84	Piet Dankert (Netherlands)
1954–56	Giuseppe Pella (Italy)	1984–87	Pierre Pflimin (France)
1956–58	Hans Furler (Germany)	1987–89	Lord Plumb (UK)
1958–60	Robert Schuman (France)	1989–92	Enrique Baron Crespo (Spain)
1960–62	Hans Furler (Germany)		
1962–64	Gaetano Martino (Italy)	1992–94	Egon A. Klepsch (Germany)
1964–65	Jean Duvieusart (Belgium)	1994–97	Klaus Hansch (Germany)
1965–66	Victor Leemans (Belgium)	1997–99	Jose Maria Gil-Robles (Spain)
1966–69	Alain Poher (France)		
1969–71	Mario Scelba (Italy)	1999–2002	Nicole Fontaine (France)
1971–73	Walter Behrendt (Germany)	2002–04	Pat Cox (Ireland)
1973–75	Cornelius Berkhouwer (Netherlands)	2004–07	Josep Borrell (Spain)
		2007–09	Hans-Gert Pöttering (Germany)
1975–77	Georges Spenale (France)		
1977–79	Emilio Colombo (Italy)		

LEADERS OF THE COMMUNIST PARTY OF THE SOVIET UNION (1922-1991)*

1922–53	Iosif Vissarionovich Stalin
1953–64	Nikita Sergeyevich Khrushchev
1964–82	Leonid Ilyich Brezhnev
1982–84	Yuriy Vladimirovich Andropov
1984–85	Konstantin Ustinovich Chernenko
1985–91	Mikhail Sergeyevich Gorbachev

* From 1898 to 1918 known as Russian Social Democratic Workers' Party (Bolshevik); from 1918 to 1925 as Russian Communist Party; from 1925 to 1952 as All-Union Communist Party.

Lenin, regardless of being the party leader to his death in Jan 1924, was never general secretary of the Central Committee nor chairman of the Politburo.

ARCHBISHOPS OF CANTERBURY

Since the English Reformation

YEAR APPOINTED

1533	Thomas Cranmer	1768	Frederick Cornwallis
1556	Reginald Pole	1783	John Moore
1559	Matthew Parker	1805	Charles Manners-Sutton
1576	Edmund Grindal	1828	William Howley
1583	John Whitgift	1848	John Bird Sumner
1604	Richard Bancroft	1862	Charles Longley
1611	George Abbot	1868	Archibald Campbell Tait
1633	William Laud	1883	Edward White Benson
1660	William Juxon	1896	Frederick Temple
1663	Gilbert Sheldon	1903	Randall Davidson
1678	William Sancroft	1928	Cosmo Lang
1691	John Tillotson	1942	William Temple
1695	Thomas Tenison	1945	Geoffrey Fisher
1716	William Wake	1961	Michael Ramsey
1737	John Potter	1974	Donald Coggan
1747	Thomas Herring	1980	Robert Runcie
1757	Matthew Hutton	1991	George Carey
1758	Thomas Secker	2002	Rowan Williams

POPES

Since the English Reformation

YEAR ELECTED

1523	Clement VII	1605	Leo XI
1534	Paul III	1605	Paul V
1550	Julius III	1621	Gregory XV
1555	Marcellus II	1623	Urban VIII
1555	Paul IV	1644	Innocent X
1559	Pius IV	1655	Alexander VII
1566	St Pius V	1667	Clement IX
1572	Gregory XIII	1670	Clement X
1585	Sixtus V	1676	Innocent XI
1590	Urban VII	1689	Alexander VIII
1590	Gregory XIV	1691	Innocent XII
1591	Innocent IX	1700	Clement XI
1592	Clement VIII	1721	Innocent XIII
		1724	Benedict XIII

1730	Clement XII	1878	Leo XIII
1740	Benedict XIV	1903	St Pius X
1758	Clement XIII	1914	Benedict XV
1769	Clement XIV	1922	Pius XI
1775	Pius VI	1939	Pius XII
1800	Pius VII	1958	John XXIII
1823	Leo XII	1963	Paul VI
1829	Pius VIII	1978	John Paul I
1831	Gregory XVI	1978	John Paul II
1846	Pius IX	2005	Benedict XVI

PATRON SAINTS

OCCUPATION	SAINT
Accountants	Matthew the Apostle
Animals (sick)	Nicholas of Tolentino
Animals (domestic)	Antony the Abbot
Archaeologists	Damasus
Architects	Thomas the Apostle
Armies	Maurice
Artists	Luke the Apostle
Astronauts	Joseph of Cupertino
Astronomers	Dominic de Guzman
Barbers	Cosmas and Damian
Booksellers	John of God
Brewers	Amand
Bricklayers	Stephen of Hungary
Builders	Thomas the Apostle
Civil Servants	Thomas More
Cooks	Lawrence
Dentists	Apollonia
Doctors	Luke the Apostle
Engineers	Ferdinand III of Castille
Farmers	Isidore the Farmer
Fishermen	Peter the Apostle
Hairdressers	Cosmas and Damian
Lawyers	Raymond of Penyafort
Midwives	Raymund Nonnatus
Mountaineers	Bernard of Menthon
Nurses	Camillus of Lellis
Paratroopers	Michael the Archangel
Policemen	Michael the Archangel
Prison officers	Hyppolitus
Publishers	John the Apostle
Sailors	Erasmus
Scholars	Thomas Aquinas
Scientists	Albertus Magnus
Singers	Cecilia
Swimmers	Adjutor
Taxi drivers	Fiacre
Teachers	John Baptist de la Salle
Travellers	Christopher
Wine merchants	Amand
Writers	Francis de Sales

COUNTRY	SAINT
England	George
Wales	David
Scotland	Andrew
N. Ireland	Patrick

ROMAN EMPERORS

Augustus	27 BC–AD 14
Tiberius	14–37
Gaius Caesar (Caligula)	37–41
Claudius I	41–54
Nero	54–68
Galba	68–69
Otho	69
Vespasian	69–79
Titus	79–81
Domitian	81–96
Nerva	96–98
Trajan	98–117
Hadrian	117–38
Antoninus Pius	138–61
Marcus Aurelius	161–80
Lucius Verus	161–69
Commodus	180–92
Pertinax	193
Didius Julianus	193
Septimius Severus	193–211
Caracalla	211–17
Geta	211–12
Macrinus	217–18
Heliogabalus	218–22
Alexander Severus	222–35
Maximin	235–38
Balbinus	238
Gordian I	238
Gordian II	238
Pupienus	238
Gordian III	238–44
Philip	244–49
Decius	249–51
Hostilianus	251
Gallus	251–53
Aemilianus	253
Valerian	253–60
Gallienus	235–68
Claudius II	268–70
Aurelian	270–75
Tacitus	275–76
Florianus	276
Probus	276–82
Carus	282–83
Carinus	283–85
Numerianus	283–84
Diocletian	284–305
Maximian	286–305
Constantius I	305–6
Galerius	305–10
Maximin	308–13
Licinius	308–24
Maxentius	306–12
Constantine I	306–37
Constantine II	337–61
Constans	337–50
Magnentius	350–53
Julian	361–63
Jovian	363–64
Valentinian I	364–75
Valens	364–78
Grantian	375–83
Maximus	383–88
Valentinian II	375–92
Eugenius	392–94
Theodosius I	375–95
Arcadius	395–408
Theodosius II	408–50
Marcian	450–57

Leo I	457–74
Leo II	474

INVENTIONS AND INVENTORS

Aeroplane	Orville and Wilbur Wright (1903)
Anaesthesia	William Morton (1846)
Aqualung	Jacques Cousteau and Emile Gagnan (1943)
Ball-point pen	Laszlo Biró (1938)
Battery	Alessandro Volta (1800)
Bifocal lens	Benjamin Franklin (1780)
Bikini	Louis Reard (1946)
Bunsen burner	Robert Wilhelm Bunsen (1855)
Burglar alarm	Edwin T. Holmes (1858)
Car (petrol driven)	Karl Benz (1886)
Cats' eyes	Percy Shaw (1934)
Cellophane	Dr Jacques Brandenberger (1908)
Centigrade thermometer	Anders Celsius (1742)
Chocolate (solid)	François-Louis Cailler (1819)
Coca-cola	John Pemberton (1886)
Computer	Charles Babbage (1835)
Condom	Gabriel Fallopius (1560)
Contact lenses	Adolph E. Fick (1887)
Contraceptive pill	Dr Gregory Pincus (1950)
Credit card	Ralph Scheider (1950)
Crossword puzzle	Arthur Wynne (1913)
Dry-cleaning	M. Jolly-Bellin (1849)
Elastic bands	Stephen Perry (1845)
Electric chair	Harold Brown and E. A. Kenneally (1890)
Fax machine	Arthur Korn (1907)
Fingerprint classification	Francis Galton (1891)
Foam rubber	John Boyd Dunlop (1929)
Fountain pen	Lewis Edson Waterman (1884)
Frozen food	Clarence Birdseye (1930)
Gyroscope	Leon Foucault (1852)
Hovercraft	Christopher Cockerell (1955)
Ice-cream cone	Italo Marcioni (1896)
Jeans	Levi Strauss (1850)
Jigsaw puzzle	George Spilsbury (1767)
Locomotive	Richard Trevithick (1804)
Machine gun	James Puckle (1718)
Microchip	Jack Saint Clair Kilby (1958)
Microwave oven	Percy Le Baron Spencer (1945)
Monopoly	Charles Darrow (1931)

Motorcycle	Gottlieb Daimler (1885)
Non-stick pan	Marc Gregoir (1954)
Paper clip	Johan Vaaler (1900)
Parking meter	Carlton Magee (1935)
Penicillin	Sir Alexander Fleming (1928)
Periodic table	Dmitry Mendeleyev (1869)
Potato crisps	George Crum (1853)
Razor (safety)	King Camp Gillette (1895)
Revolver	Samuel Colt (1835)
Roller skates	Joseph Merlin (1760)
Roulette wheel	Blaise Pascal (1647)
Safety pin	Walter Hunt (1849)
Scrabble	James Brunot (1950)
Stapler	Charles Henry Gould (1868)
Tampon	Earl Hass (1930)
Thermometer	Galileo Galilei (1593)
Toothbrush	William Addis (1649)
Travel agency	Thomas Cook (1841)
Vaccination	Edward Jenner (1770)
Xerox copier	Chester Carlson (1938)
X-ray	Wilhelm Konrad Rontgen (1895)
Zip fastener	Whitcomb L. Judson (1891)

PLACES

COUNTRIES OF THE WORLD

COUNTRY	AREA (SQ. KM)	POPULATION (MILLIONS)	CAPITAL
AFGHANISTAN	647,500	31,056,997	Kabul
ALBANIA	28,748	3,581,655	Tirana
ALGERIA	2,381,740	32,930,091	Algiers
ANDORRA	468	71,201	Andorra la Vella
ANGOLA	1,246,700	12,127,071	Luanda
ANTIGUA AND BARBUDA	443	69,108	St John's
ARGENTINA	2,766,890	39,921,833	Buenos Aires
ARMENIA	29,800	2,976,372	Yerevan
AUSTRALIA	7,686,850	20,264,082	Canberra
AUSTRIA	83,870	8,192,880	Vienna
AZERBAIJAN	86,600	7,961,619	Baki (Baku)
THE BAHAMAS	13,940	303,770	Nassau
BAHRAIN	665	698,585	Manama
BANGLADESH	144,000	147,365,352	Dhaka
BARBADOS	431	279,912	Bridgetown
BELARUS	207,600	10,293,011	Minsk
BELGIUM	30,528	10,379,067	Brussels
BELIZE	22,966	287,730	Belmopan
BENIN	112,620	7,862,944	Porto Novo
BHUTAN	47,000	2,279,723	Thimphu
BOLIVIA	1,098,580	8,989,046	La Paz
BOSNIA AND HERCEGOVINA	51,129	4,498,976	Sarajevo
BOTSWANA	600,370	1,639,833	Gaborone
BRAZIL	8,511,965	188,078,227	Brasília
BRUNEI	5,770	379,444	Bandar Seri Begawan
BULGARIA	110,910	7,385,367	Sofia
BURKINA FASO	274,200	13,902,972	Ouagadougou
BURUNDI	27,830	8,090,068	Bujumbura
CAMBODIA	181,040	13,881,427	Phnom Penh
CAMEROON	475,440	17,340,702	Yaoundé
CANADA	9,984,670	33,098,932	Ottawa

COUNTRY	AREA (SQ. KM)	POPULATION (MILLIONS)	CAPITAL
CAPE VERDE	4,033	420,979	Praia
CENTRAL AFRICAN REP.	622,984	4,303,356	Bangui
CHAD	1,284,000	9,944,201	N'Djaména
CHILE	756,950	6,134,219	Santiago
CHINA	9,596,960	1,313,973,713	Beijing
COLOMBIA	1,138,910	43,593,035	Bogotá
THE COMOROS	2,170	690,948	Moroni
DEMOCRATIC REP. OF CONGO	2,345,410	62,660,551	Kinshasa
REP. OF CONGO	342,000	3,702,314	Brazzaville
COSTA RICA	51,100	4,075,261	San José
CÔTE D'IVOIRE	322,460	17,654,843	Yamoussoukro
CROATIA	56,542	4,494,749	Zagreb
CUBA	110,860	11,382,820	Havana
CYPRUS	9,250	784,301	Nicosia
CZECH REPUBLIC	78,866	10,235,455	Prague
DENMARK	43,094	5,450,661	Copenhagen
DJIBOUTI	23,000	486,530	Djibouti
DOMINICA	754	68,910	Roseau
DOMINICAN REPUBLIC	48,730	9,183,984	Santo Domingo
EAST TIMOR	15,007	1,062,777	Dili
ECUADOR	283,560	13,547,510	Quito
EGYPT	1,001,450	78,887,007	Cairo
EL SALVADOR	21,040	6,822,378	San Salvador
EQUATORIAL GUINEA	28,051	540,109	Malabo
ERITREA	121,320	4,786,994	Asmara
ESTONIA	45,226	1,324,333	Tallinn
ETHIOPIA	1,127,127	74,777,981	Addis Ababa
FIJI	18,270	905,949	Suva
FINLAND	338,145	5,231,372	Helsinki
FRANCE	547,030	60,876,136	Paris
GABON	267,667	1,424,906	Libreville
THE GAMBIA	11,300	1,641,564	Banjul
GEORGIA	69,700	4,661,473	Tbilisi
GERMANY	357,021	82,422,299	Berlin

COUNTRY	AREA (SQ. KM)	POPULATION (MILLIONS)	CAPITAL
GHANA	239,460	22,409,572	Accra
GREECE	131,940	10,688,058	Athens
GRENADA	344	89,703	St George's
GUATEMALA	108,890	12,293,545	Guatemala City
GUINEA	245,857	9,690,222	Conakry
GUINEA-BISSAU	36,120	1,442,029	Bissau
GUYANA	214,970	767,245	Georgetown
HAITI	27,750	8,308,504	Port-au-Prince
HONDURAS	112,090	7,326,496	Tegucigalpa
HUNGARY	92,030	9,981,334	Budapest
ICELAND	103,000	299,388	Reykjavik
INDIA	3,287,590	1,095,351,995	New Delhi
INDONESIA	1,919,440	245,452,739	Jakarta
IRAN	1,648,000	68,688,433	Tehran
IRAQ	437,072	26,783,383	Baghdad
IRELAND	70,280	4,062,235	Dublin
ISRAEL AND PALESTINIAN TERRITORIES	20,770	6,352,117	Tel Aviv
ITALY	301,230	58,133,509	Rome
JAMAICA	10,991	2,758,124	Kingston
JAPAN	377,835	127,463,611	Tokyo
JORDAN	92,300	5,906,760	Amman
KAZAKHSTAN	2,717,300	15,233,244	Astana
KENYA	582,650	34,707,817	Nairobi
KIRIBATI	811	105,432	Tarawa
DEM. PEOPLE'S REP. OF KOREA	120,540	23,113,019	Pyongyang
REP. OF KOREA	98,480	48,846,823	Seoul
KUWAIT	17,820	2,418,393	Kuwait City
KYRGYZSTAN	198,000	5,213,898	Bishkek
LAOS	236,800	6,368,481	Vientiane
LATVIA	64,589	2,274,735	Riga
LEBANON	10,400	3,874,050	Beirut
LESOTHO	30,355	2,022,331	Maseru
LIBERIA	111,370	3,042,004	Monrovia
LIBYA	1,759,500	5,900,754	Tripoli
LIECHTENSTEIN	160	33,987	Vaduz

COUNTRY	AREA (SQ. KM)	POPULATION (MILLIONS)	CAPITAL
LITHUANIA	65,200	3,585,906	Vilnius
LUXEMBOURG	2,586	474,413	Luxembourg
MACEDONIA	25,333	2,050,554	Skopje
MADAGASCAR	587,040	18,595,469	Antananarivo
MALAWI	118,480	13,013,926	Lilongwe
MALAYSIA	329,750	24,385,858	Kuala Lumpur
MALDIVES	300	359,008	Male
MALI	1,240,000	11,716,829	Bamako
MALTA	316	400,214	Valletta
MARSHALL ISLANDS	11,854	60,422	Dalap-Uliga-Darrit
MAURITANIA	1,030,700	3,177,388	Nouakchott
MAURITIUS	2,040	1,240,827	Port Louis
MEXICO	1,972,550	107,449,525	Mexico City
FED. STATES OF MICRONESIA	702	108,004	Palikir
MOLDOVA	33,843	4,466,706	Chisinau
MONACO	1.95	32,543	Monaco
MONGOLIA	1,564,116	2,832,224	Ulaanbaatar
MONTENEGRO	14,026	630,548	Podgorica
MOROCCO	446,550	33,241,259	Rabat
MOZAMBIQUE	801,590	19,686,505	Maputo
MYANMAR	676,500	47,382,633	Naypyidaw
NAMIBIA	825,418	2,044,147	Windhoek
NAURU	21	13,287	Yaren District
NEPAL	147,181	28,287,147	Kathmandu
THE NETHERLANDS	41,526	16,491,461	Amsterdam
NEW ZEALAND	268,680	4,076,140	Wellington
NICARAGUA	129,494	5,570,129	Managua
NIGERIA	923,768	131,859,731	Abuja
NIGER	1,267,000	12,525,094	Niamey
NORWAY	323,802	4,610,820	Oslo
OMAN	212,460	3,102,229	Muscat (Masqat)
PAKISTAN	803,940	165,803,560	Islamabad
PALAU	458	20,579	Melekeok
PANAMA	78,200	3,191,319	Panama City
PAPUA NEW GUINEA	462,840	5,670,544	Port Moresby

COUNTRY	AREA (SQ. KM)	POPULATION (MILLIONS)	CAPITAL
PARAGUAY	406,750	6,506,464	Asunción
PERU	1,285,220	28,302,603	Lima
THE PHILIPPINES	300,000	89,468,677	Manila
POLAND	312,685	38,536,869	Warsaw
PORTUGAL	92,391	10,605,870	Lisbon
QATAR	11,437	885,359	Doha
ROMANIA	237,500	22,303,552	Bucharest
RUSSIAN FEDERATION	17,075,200	142,893,540	Moscow
RWANDA	26,338	8,648,248	Kigali
ST CHRISTOPHER AND NEVIS	261	39,129	Basseterre
ST LUCIA	616	168,458	Castries
ST VINCENT AND THE GRENADINES	389	117,848	Kingstown
SAMOA	2,944	176,908	Apia
SAN MARINO	61.2	29,251	San Marino
SAO TOME AND PRINCIPE	1,001	193,413	Sao Tome
SAUDI ARABIA	1,960,582	27,019,731	Riyadh
SENEGAL	196,190	11,987,121	Dakar
SERBIA	88,361	9,396,411	Belgrade
SEYCHELLES	455	81,541	Victoria
SIERRA LEONE	71,740	6,005,250	Freetown
SINGAPORE	692.7	4,492,150	Singapore
SLOVAKIA	48,845	5,439,448	Bratislava
SLOVENIA	20,273	2,010,347	Ljubljana
SOLOMON ISLANDS	28,450	552,438	Honiara
SOMALIA	637,657	8,863,338	Mogadishu
SOUTH AFRICA	1,219,912	44,187,637	Tshwane/ Cape Town/ Bloemfontein
SPAIN	504,782	40,397,842	Madrid
SRI LANKA	65,610	20,222,240	Colombo/Sri Jayewardenepura Kotte
SUDAN	2,505,810	41,236,378	Khartoum
SURINAME	163,270	439,117	Paramaribo

COUNTRY	AREA (SQ. KM)	POPULATION (MILLIONS)	CAPITAL
SWAZILAND	17,363	1,136,334	Mbabane
SWEDEN	449,964	9,016,596	Stockholm
SWITZERLAND	41,290	7,523,934	Bern
SYRIA	185,180	18,881,361	Damascus
TAIWAN	35,980	23,036,087	Taipei
TAJIKISTAN	143,100	7,320,815	Dushanbe
TANZANIA	945,087	37,445,392	Dodoma
THAILAND	514,000	64,631,595	Bangkok
TOGO	56,785	5,548,702	Lomé
TONGA	748	114,689	Nuku'alofa
TRINIDAD AND TOBAGO	5,128	1,065,842	Port of Spain
TUNISIA	163,610	10,175,014	Tunis
TURKEY	780,580	70,413,958	Ankara
TURKMENISTAN	488,100	5,042,920	Ashgabat
TUVALU	26	11,810	Funafuti
UGANDA	236,040	28,195,754	Kampala
UKRAINE	603,700	46,710,816	Kyiv
UNITED ARAB EMIRATES	82,880	2,602,713	Abu Dhabi
UNITED KINGDOM	242,514	60,441,457	London
UNITED STATES OF AMERICA	9,631,420	298,444,215	Washington DC
URUGUAY	176,220	3,431,932	Montevideo
UZBEKISTAN	447,400	27,307,134	Tashkent
VANUATU	12,200	208,869	Port Vila
VATICAN CITY STATE	0.44	921	Vatican City
VENEZUELA	912,050	25,730,435	Caracas
VIETNAM	329,560	84,402,966	Hanoi
YEMEN	527,970	21,456,188	Sana'a
ZAMBIA	754,614	11,502,010	Lusaka
ZIMBABWE	390,580	12,236,805	Harare

STATES OF THE USA

STATE (DATE AND ORDER OF ADMISSION)	ABBREVIATION	CAPITAL
Alabama (1819, 22)	AL	Montgomery
Alaska (1959, 49)	AK	Juneau
Arizona (1912, 48)	AZ	Phoenix
Arkansas (1836, 25)	AR	Little Rock
California (1850, 31)	CA	Sacramento
Colorado (1876, 38)	CO	Denver
Connecticut* (1788, 5)	CT	Hartford
Delaware* (1787, 1)	DE	Dover
District of Columbia (1791)	DC	—
Florida (1845, 27)	FL	Tallahassee
Georgia* (1788, 4)	GA	Atlanta
Hawaii (1959, 50)	HI	Honolulu
Idaho (1890, 43)	ID	Boise
Illinois (1818, 21)	IL	Springfield
Indiana (1816, 19)	IN	Indianapolis
Iowa (1846, 29)	IA	Des Moines
Kansas (1861, 34)	KS	Topeka
Kentucky (1792, 15)	KY	Frankfort
Louisiana (1812, 18)	LA	Baton Rouge
Maine (1820, 23)	ME	Augusta
Maryland* (1788, 7)	MD	Annapolis
Massachusetts* (1788, 6)	MA	Boston
Michigan (1837, 26)	MI	Lansing
Minnesota (1858, 32)	MN	St Paul
Mississippi (1817, 20)	MS	Jackson
Missouri (1821, 24)	MO	Jefferson City
Montana (1889, 41)	MT	Helena
Nebraska (1867, 37)	NE	Lincoln
Nevada (1864, 36)	NV	Carson City
New Hampshire* (1788, 9)	NH	Concord
New Jersey* (1787, 3)	NJ	Trenton
New Mexico (1912, 47)	NM	Santa Fé
New York* (1788, 11)	NY	Albany
North Carolina* (1789, 12)	NC	Raleigh
North Dakota (1889, 39)	ND	Bismarck
Ohio (1803, 17)	OH	Columbus

STATE (DATE AND ORDER OF ADMISSION)	ABBREVIATION	CAPITAL
Oklahoma (1907, 46)	OK	Oklahoma City
Oregon (1859, 33)	OR	Salem
Pennsylvania* (1787, 2)	PA	Harrisburg
Rhode Island* (1790, 13)	RI	Providence
South Carolina* (1788, 8)	SC	Columbia
South Dakota (1889, 40)	SD	Pierre
Tennessee (1796, 16)	TN	Nashville
Texas (1845, 28)	TX	Austin
Utah (1896, 45)	UT	Salt Lake City
Vermont (1791, 14)	VT	Montpelier
Virginia* (1788, 10)	VA	Richmond
Washington (1889, 42)	WA	Olympia
West Virginia (1863, 35)	WV	Charleston
Wisconsin (1848, 30)	WI	Madison
Wyoming (1890, 44)	WY	Cheyenne

*The 13 original states

STATES AND TERRITORIES OF AUSTRALIA

	ABBREVIATION	CAPITAL
Australian Capital Territory	ACT	Canberra
New South Wales	NSW	Sydney
Northern Territory	NT	Darwin
Queensland	Qld	Brisbane
South Australia	SA	Adelaide
Tasmania	Tas.	Hobart
Victoria	Vic.	Melbourne
Western Australia	WA	Perth

PROVINCES AND TERRITORIES OF CANADA

	ABBREVIATION	CAPITAL
Alberta	AB	Edmonton
British Columbia	BC	Victoria
Manitoba	MB	Winnipeg
New Brunswick	NB	Fredericton
Newfoundland and Labrador	NF	St John's
Northwest Territories	NT	Yellowknife
Nova Scotia	NS	Halifax

	ABBREVIATION	CAPITAL
Nunavut	NT	Iqaluit
Ontario	ON	Toronto
Prince Edward Island	PE	Charlottetown
Quebec	QC	Quebec City
Saskatchewan	SK	Regina
Yukon Territory	YT	Whitehorse

UNITED NATIONS MEMBER STATES

Afghanistan; Albania; Algeria; Andorra; Angola; Antigua and Barbuda; Argentina; Armenia; Australia; Austria; Azerbaijan; Bahamas; Bahrain; Bangladesh; Barbados; Belarus; Belgium; Belize; Benin; Bhutan; Bolivia; Bosnia and Hercegovina; Botswana; Brazil; Brunei; Bulgaria; Burkina Faso; Burundi; Cambodia; Cameroon; Canada; Cape Verde; Central African Republic; Chad; Chile; China; Colombia; Comoros; Congo, Dem. Rep. of; Congo, Rep. of; Costa Rica; Côte d'Ivoire; Croatia; Cuba; Cyprus; Czech Republic; Denmark; Djibouti; Dominica; Dominican Republic; East Timor; Ecuador; Egypt; El Salvador; Equatorial Guinea; Eritrea; Estonia; Ethiopia; Fiji; Finland; France; Gabon; Gambia; Georgia; Germany; Ghana; Greece; Grenada; Guatemala; Guinea; Guinea-Bissau; Guyana; Haiti; Honduras; Hungary; Iceland; India; Indonesia; Iran; Iraq; Ireland; Israel; Italy; Jamaica; Japan; Jordan; Kazakhstan; Kenya; Kiribati; Korea, Dem. Rep. of; Korea, Rep. of; Kuwait; Kyrgyzstan; Laos; Latvia; Lebanon; Lesotho; Liberia; Libya; Liechtenstein; Lithuania; Luxembourg; FYR Macedonia; Madagascar; Malawi; Malaysia; Maldives; Mali; Malta; Marshall Islands; Mauritania; Mauritius; Mexico; Micronesia (Federated States of); Moldova; Monaco; Mongolia; Montenegro; Morocco; Mozambique; Myanmar; Namibia; Nauru; Nepal; Netherlands; New Zealand; Nicaragua; Niger; Nigeria; Norway; Oman; Pakistan; Palau; Panama; Papua New Guinea; Paraguay; Peru; Philippines; Poland; Portugal; Qatar; Romania; Russian Federation; Rwanda; Saint Kitts and Nevis; Saint Lucia; Saint Vincent and the Grenadines; Samoa; San Marino; Sao Tome and Principe; Saudi Arabia; Senegal; Serbia; Seychelles; Sierra Leone; Singapore; Slovakia; Slovenia; Solomon Islands; Somalia; South Africa; Spain; Sri Lanka; Sudan; Suriname; Swaziland; Sweden; Switzerland; Syria; Tajikistan; Tanzania; Thailand; Togo; Tonga; Trinidad and Tobago; Tunisia; Turkey; Turkmenistan; Tuvalu; Uganda; Ukraine; United Arab Emirates; United Kingdom; United States of America; Uruguay; Uzbekistan; Vanuatu; Venezuela; Vietnam; Yemen; Zambia; Zimbabwe.

MEMBERS OF THE COMMONWEALTH

COUNTRY (YEAR JOINED)

Antigua and Barbuda (1981)
Australia (1931)
The Bahamas (1973)
Bangladesh (1972)
Barbados (1966)
Belize (1981)
Botswana (1966)
Brunei (1984)
Cameroon (1995)
Canada (1931)
Cyprus (1961)
Dominica (1978)
Fiji (1970, currently suspended)
The Gambia (1965)
Ghana (1957)
Grenada (1974)
Guyana (1966)
India (1947)
Jamaica (1962)
Kenya (1963)
Kiribati (1979)
Lesotho (1966)
Malawi (1964)
Malaysia (1957)
The Maldives (1982)
Malta (1964)
Mauritius (1968)
Mozambique (1995)
Namibia (1990)
Nauru (1968)
New Zealand (1931)
Nigeria (1960)
Pakistan (1947)
Papua New Guinea (1975)
St Kitts and Nevis (1983)
St Lucia (1979)
St Vincent and the Grenadines (1979)

Samoa (1970)
Seychelles (1976)
Sierra Leone (1961)
Singapore (1965)
Solomon Islands (1978)
South Africa (1931)
Sri Lanka (1948)
Swaziland (1968)
Tanzania (1961)
Tonga (1970)
Trinidad and Tobago (1962)
Tuvalu (1978)
Uganda (1962)
United Kingdom
Vanuatu (1980)
Zambia (1964)

CITIES ON RIVERS

CITY	RIVER
Amsterdam	Amstel
Antwerp	Scheldt
Baghdad	Tigris
Bangkok	Chao Phraya
Basle	Rhine
Belfast	Lagan
Belgrade	Danube
Bonn	Rhine
Bordeaux	Garonne
Bristol	Avon
Brussels	Senne
Bucharest	Dimbovita
Budapest	Danube
Buenos Aires	Rio de la Plata
Cairo	Nile
Calcutta	Hooghly
Cambridge	Cam
Cologne	Rhine
Dublin	Liffey
Florence	Arno

Frankfurt	Main
Hamburg	Elbe
Kyiv	Dnieper
Lisbon	Tagus
London	Thames
Lyons	Rhone
Madrid	Manzanares
Melbourne	Yarra
Moscow	Moskva
New Orleans	Mississippi
New York	Hudson
Paris	Seine
Perth	Swan
Pisa	Arno
Prague	Vltava
Shanghai	Yangtze
Vienna	Danube
Warsaw	Vistula
Washington	Potomac

LONDON

DISTANCES FROM LONDON BY AIR

This list details the distances in miles from Heathrow Airport in London to various cities abroad.

TO	KM	MILES
Abu Dhabi	5,512	3,425
Acapulco	9,177	5,702
Accra	5,097	3,167
Addis Ababa	5,915	3,675
Adelaide	16,283	10,111
Aden	5,907	3,670
Alexandria	3,350	2,082
Algiers	1,666	1,035
Amman	3,681	2,287
Amsterdam	370	230
Anchorage	7,196	4,472

TO	KM	MILES
Ankara	2,848	1,770
Atlanta	6,756	4,198
Auckland	18,353	11,404
Bali	12,518	7,779
Bangkok	9,540	5,928
Barcelona	1,146	712
Beijing	8,148	5,063
Beirut	3,478	2,161
Belfast	524	325
Belgrade	1,700	1,056
Belize City	8,340	5,182
Benghazi	2,734	1,699
Berlin	947	588
Bogotá	8,468	5,262
Boston	5,239	3,255
Brasília	8,775	5,452
Bratislava	1,315	817
Brazzaville	6,368	3,957
Bridgetown	6,748	4,193
Brisbane	16,533	10,273
Brussels	349	217
Bucharest	2,103	1,307
Budapest	1,486	923
Buenos Aires	11,129	6,915
Cairo	3,531	2,194
Calgary	7,012	4,357
Canberra	16,999	10,563
Cape Town	9,675	6,011
Caracas	7,466	4,639
Casablanca	2,092	1,300
Chennai/Madras	8,229	5,113
Chicago	6,343	3,941
Cologne/Bonn	533	331
Colombo	8,708	5,411
Copenhagen	978	608
Dallas-Fort Worth	7,622	4,736
Damascus	3,577	2,223
Dar es Salaam	7,502	4,662
Darwin	13,861	8,613
Denver	7,492	4,655

TO	KM	MILES	TO	KM	MILES
Dhaka	8,008	4,976	Kolkata/Calcutta	7,979	4,958
Doha	5,235	3,253	Kraków	1,425	886
Douala	5,356	3,328	Kuala Lumpur	10,552	6,557
Dresden	987	613	Kuwait	4,671	2,903
Dubai	5,494	3,414	Lagos	5,000	3,107
Dublin	449	279	Larnaca	3,276	2,036
Dubrovnik	1,727	1,073	Las Palmas	2,897	1,800
Dundee	579	359	Lisbon	1,564	972
Durban	9,555	5,937	Ljubljana	1,233	767
Düsseldorf	500	310	Lomé	5,036	3,129
Edmonton	6,805	4,229	Los Angeles	8,753	5,439
Frankfurt	653	406	Luanda	6,830	4,243
Gaborone	8,842	5,494	Lusaka	7,933	4,929
Geneva	754	468	Luxor	3,999	2,485
Glasgow	555	345	Lyon-Bron	750	466
Guatemala City	8,745	5,435	Madrid	1,244	773
Hamburg	745	463	Málaga	1,675	1,041
Hannover	703	437	Malé	8,533	5,302
Harare	8,298	5,156	Malmö-Sturup	1,017	632
Havana	7,479	4,647	Malta	2,100	1,305
Helsinki	1,847	1,147	Manila	10,758	6,685
Ho Chi Minh City	10,211	6,345	Maputo	9,184	5,707
Hong Kong	9,640	5,990	Marrakech-Menara	2,292	1,424
Honolulu	11,619	7,220	Marseille	988	614
Houston	7,759	4,821	Melbourne	16,897	10,499
Islamabad	6,062	3,767	Memphis	7,005	4,353
Isle of Man	403	250	Menorca	1,339	832
Istanbul	2,510	1,560	Mexico City	8,899	5,529
Jakarta	11,741	7,295	Miami	7,104	4,414
Jeddah	4,743	2,947	Milan	979	609
Johannesburg	9,068	5,634	Minneapolis-St Paul	6,439	4,001
Kabul	5,726	3,558	Minsk	1,893	1,176
Karachi	6,334	3,935	Mombasa	7,236	4,497
Kathmandu	7,354	4,570	Montego Bay	7,544	4,687
Khartoum	4,943	3,071	Montevideo	11,010	6,841
Kiev	2,184	1,357	Montréal	5,213	3,239
Kigali	6,600	4,101	Moscow	2,506	1,557
Kilimanjaro	7,055	4,384	Mumbai/Bombay	7,207	4,478
Kingston, Jamaica	7,513	4,668	Munich	940	584
Kinshasa	6,387	3,969	Muscat	5,828	3,621

TO	KM	MILES	TO	KM	MILES
Naples	1,628	1,011	San Francisco	8,610	5,351
Nassau	6,973	4,333	São Paulo	9,483	5,892
Natal	7,180	4,462	Sarajevo	1,636	1,017
N'Djamena	4,588	2,851	Seoul	8,863	5,507
Newark	5,558	3,454	Seychelles	8,169	5,076
New Delhi	6,727	4,180	Shannon	594	369
New York	5,536	3,440	Shetland Islands	936	582
Nice	1,039	645	Singapore	10,873	6,756
Novosibirsk	5,216	3,241	Skopje	1,963	1,220
Orlando	6,954	4,321	Sofia	2,038	1,266
Osaka	9,498	5,901	Split	1,530	951
Oslo	1,206	749	Stockholm	1,461	908
Ostend-Bruges	232	144	Strasbourg	663	412
Ottawa	5,344	3,321	Stuttgart	754	469
Ouagadougou	4,348	2,702	Suva	16,285	10,119
Palma de Mallorca	1,347	836	Sydney	17,008	10,568
Panama City	8,448	5,249	Tahiti	15,361	9,545
Paris	346	215	Taipei	9,775	6,074
Penang	10,277	6,386	Tbilisi	3,571	2,219
Perth, Australia	14,497	9,008	Tehran	4,411	2,741
Philadelphia	5,686	3,533	Tel Aviv	3,585	2,227
Pisa	1,184	736	Thessaloniki	2,164	1,345
Port of Spain	7,088	4,404	Tokyo	9,585	5,956
Prague	1,043	649	Toronto	5,704	3,544
Québec	4,979	3,093	Treviso	1,130	703
Quito	9,188	5,709	Tripoli	2,362	1,468
Rabat	2,001	1,243	Trondheim	1,490	926
Rangoon/Yangon	8,984	5,582	Tunis-Carthage	1,830	1,137
Reykjavik	1,895	1,177	Turin	917	570
Rhodes	2,805	1,743	Ulaanbaatar	6,984	4,340
Riga	1,695	1,054	Vancouver	7,574	4,707
Rimini	1,275	793	Venice	1,150	715
Rio de Janeiro	9,245	5,745	Vienna	1,272	790
Riyadh	4,936	3,067	Vladivostok	8,526	5,298
Rome	1,441	895	Warsaw	1,468	912
St Lucia	6,785	4,216	Washington	5,898	3,665
St Petersburg	2,114	1,314	Wellington	18,817	11,692
Salt Lake City	7,806	4,850	Zagreb	1,365	848
Salzburg	1,048	651	Zürich	787	490
San Diego	8,802	5,469			

THAMES BRIDGES

(from east to west)

Queen Elizabeth II Bridge, opened 1991
Tower Bridge, opened 1894
London Bridge, original opened 1831; current bridge opened 1973
Cannon Street Railway Bridge, opened 1866
Southwark Bridge, opened 1819
Millennium Bridge, opened 2000; reopened 2002
Blackfriars, Railway Bridge, opened 1864, only the columns remain
Blackfriars Bridge, opened 1769
Waterloo Bridge, opened 1817
Golden Jubilee Bridges, opened 2002
Hungerford Railway Bridge, opened 1845
Westminster Bridge, opened 1750
Lambeth Bridge, opened 1862
Vauxhall Bridge, opened 1816
Grosvenor Bridge, opened 1860
Chelsea Bridge, opened 1858
Albert Bridge, opened 1873
Battersea Bridge, opened 1771
Battersea Railway Bridge, opened 1863
Wandsworth Bridge, opened 1873
Putney Railway Bridge, opened 1889
Putney Bridge, original opened 1729; current bridge opened 1886
Hammersmith Bridge, built 1827
Barnes Railway Bridge, opened 1849
Chiswick Bridge, opened 1933
Kew Railway Bridge, opened 1869
Kew Bridge, original built 1759; current bridge opened 1903
Richmond Lock, opened 1894
Twickenham Bridge, opened 1933
Richmond Railway Bridge, opened 1848
Richmond Bridge, built 1777
Teddington Lock, opened 1889
Kingston Railway Bridge, opened 1863
Kingston Bridge, built 1825–8
Hampton Court Bridge, built 1753

LINES OF THE LONDON UNDERGROUND

LINE (YEAR OPENED)	COLOUR
Bakerloo (1906)	brown
Central (1900)	red
Circle (1884)	yellow
District (1868)	green
East London (1869)	orange
Hammersmith and City (1863)	pink
Jubilee (1879)	silver
Metropolitan (1863)	maroon
Northern (1890)	black
Piccadilly (1906)	dark blue
Victoria (1968)	light blue
Waterloo and City (1898)	turquoise

THE UNITED KINGDOM

AREA

The United Kingdom comprises Great Britain (England, Wales and Scotland) and Northern Ireland.

The Isle of Man and the Channel Islands are Crown dependencies with their own legislative systems, and not part of the United Kingdom.

	KM²	MILES²
United Kingdom	242,495	93,627
England	130,279	50,301
Wales	20,733	8,005
Scotland	77,907	30,080
Northern Ireland*	13,576	5,242
Isle of Man	572	221
Channel Islands	194	75

*Excluding certain tidal waters that are parts of statutory areas in Northern Ireland

POPULATION

The first official census of population in England, Wales and Scotland was taken in 1801 and a census has been taken every ten years since, except in 1941 when there was no census because of war. The last official census in the United Kingdom was taken in April 2001.

The first official census of population in Ireland was taken in 1841. However, all figures given below refer only to the area which is now Northern Ireland. Figures for Northern Ireland in 1921 and 1931 are estimates based on the censuses taken in 1926 and 1937 respectively.

Estimates of the population of England before 1801, calculated from the number of baptisms, burials and marriages, are:

1570	4,160,221
1600	4,811,718
1630	5,600,517
1670	5,773,646
1700	6,045,008
1750	6,517,035

UK CENSUS RESULTS 1811–2001

	TOTAL	MALE	FEMALE
1811	13,368,000	6,368,000	7,000,000
1821	15,472,000	7,498,000	7,974,000
1831	17,835,000	8,647,000	9,188,000
1841	20,183,000	9,819,000	10,364,000
1851	22,259,000	10,855,000	11,404,000
1861	24,525,000	11,894,000	12,631,000
1871	27,431,000	13,309,000	14,122,000
1881	31,015,000	15,060,000	15,955,000
1891	34,264,000	16,593,000	17,671,000
1901	38,237,000	18,492,000	19,745,000
1911	42,082,000	20,357,000	21,725,000
1921	44,027,000	21,033,000	22,994,000
1931	46,038,000	22,060,000	23,978,000
1951	50,225,000	24,118,000	26,107,000
1961	52,709,000	25,481,000	27,228,000
1971	55,515,000	26,952,000	28,562,000
1981	55,848,000	27,104,000	28,742,000
1991	56,467,000	27,344,000	29,123,000
2001	58,789,194	28,581,233	30,207,961

POPULATION BY AGE AND SEX UK CENSUS 2001

AGE RANGE	MALES	FEMALES
	THOUSANDS	
0–4	1,786	1,700
5–9	1,915	1,823
10–14	1.988	1,893
15–19	1,871	1,793
20–24	1,765	1,781
25–29	1,896	1,972
30–34	2,200	2,294
35–39	2,278	2,348
40–44	2,057	2,095
45–49	1,851	1,885
50–54	2,003	2,037
55–59	1,651	1,687
60–64	1,410	1,470
65–69	1,241	1,355
70–74	1,059	1,280
75–79	818	1,149

AGE RANGE	MALES	FEMALES
80–84	483	831
85–89	227	526
90 and over	83	288

RELIGIONS IN THE UK

Christian	42,079,000	71.6%
Muslim	1,591,000	12.7%
Hindu	559,000	1.0%
Sikh	336,000	0.6%
Jewish	267,000	0.5%
Buddhist	152,000	0.3%
Other religion	179,000	0.3%
All religions	45,163,000	76.8%
No religion/not stated	13,626,000	23.2%
Total	58,789,000	100%

Other religions practised in the UK include the Baha'i Faith, Humanism, Jainism, Paganism, Scientology and Zoroastrianism

THE ANCIENT WORLD

THE SEVEN WONDERS OF THE WORLD

The following sights were identified by classical observers as the pre-eminent architectural and sculptural achievements of the ancient world. Only the pyramids of Egypt are still in existence.

I THE PYRAMIDS OF EGYPT
The pyramids are found from Gizeh, near Cairo, to a southern limit 96 km (60 miles) distant. The oldest is that of Zoser, at Saqqara, built c.2650 BC. The Great Pyramid of Cheops (built c.2580 BC) covers 13.12 acres (230.4 x 230.4 m or 756 x 756 ft) at the base and was originally 146.6 m (481 ft) in height.

II THE HANGING GARDENS OF BABYLON
These adjoined Nebuchadnezzar's palace, 96 km (60 miles) south of Baghdad. The terraced gardens, ranging from 25–90 m (75 ft to 300 ft) above ground level, were watered from storage tanks on the highest terrace.

III THE TOMB OF MAUSOLUS
Built at Halicarnassus, in Asia Minor, by the widowed Queen Artemisia about 350 BC. The memorial originated the term mausoleum.

IV THE TEMPLE OF ARTEMIS AT EPHESUS
Ionic temple erected about 350 BC in honour of the goddess and burned by the Goths in AD 262.

V THE COLOSSUS OF RHODES
A bronze statue of Apollo, set up about 280 BC. According to legend it stood at the harbour entrance of the seaport of Rhodes.

VI THE STATUE OF ZEUS
Located at Olympia in the plain of Elis, and constructed of marble inlaid with ivory and gold by the sculptor Phidias, about 430 BC.

VII THE PHAROS OF ALEXANDRIA
A marble watch tower and lighthouse on the island of Pharos in the harbour of Alexandria, built c.270 BC.

ROMAN NAMES

The following is a list of the Roman names for geographical areas and features and for towns and settlements. The area to which the Roman name for a town or country referred is not necessarily precisely the same area occupied by the modern town or country.

THE BRITISH ISLES

Abergavenny	*Gobannium*
Aldborough	*Isurium Brigantum*
Ambleside	*Galava*
Ancaster	*Causennae*
Anglesey	*Mona*
Armagh	*Armacha*
Avon, R.	*Auvona*
Bath	*Aquae Sulis*
Brancaster	*Branodunum*

Britain	*Britannia*	Lincoln	*Lindum*
Caerleon	*Isca*	Lizard Point	*Damnonium*
Caerwent	*Venta Silurum*		*Promunturium*
Canterbury	*Durovernum*	London	*Londinium*
	Cantiacorum	Manchester	*Mamucium*
Cardigan	*Ceretica*	Man, Isle of	*Monapia*
Carlisle	*Luguvalium*	Newcastle upon Tyne	*Pons Aelius*
Carmarthen	*Maridunum*	Orkneys	*Orcades*
Caernarvon	*Segontium*	Pevensey	*Anderetium*
Chelmsford	*Caesaromagus*	Portsmouth	*Magnus Portus*
Chester	*Deva*	Richborough	*Rutupiae*
Chichester	*Noviomagus*	Rochester	*Durobrivae*
	Regnensium	St Albans	*Verulamium*
Cirencester	*Corinium*	Salisbury (Old Sarum)	*Sorviodunum*
	Dobunnorum	Scilly Isles	*Cassiterides*
Clyde, R.	*Clota*	Scotland	*Caledonia*
Colchester	*Camulodunum*	Severn, R.	*Sabrina*
Corbridge	*Corstopitum*	Silchester	*Calleva*
Dee, R.	*Deva*		*Atrebatum*
Doncaster	*Danum*	Solway Firth	*Ituna aestuarium*
Dorchester	*Durnovaria*	Thames, R.	*Tamesis*
Dover	*Dubris*	Wales	*Cambria*
Dover, Straits of	*Fretum Gallicum*	Wallsend	*Segedunum*
Dunstable	*Durocobrivae*	Wash, The	*Metaris*
Eden, R.	*Ituna*		*aestuarium*
England	*Anglia*	Wear, R.	*Vedra*
Exeter	*Isca*	Wight, Isle of	*Vectis*
	Dumnoniorum	Winchester	*Venta Belgarum*
Forth, R.	*Bodotria*	Worcester	*Vigornia*
Gloucester	*Glevum*	Wroxeter	*Viroconium*
Hebrides	*Ebudae Insulae*		*Cornoviorum*
Hexham	*Axelodunum*	York	*Eburacum*
Ilkley	*Olicana*		
Ireland	*Hibernia*	**CONTINENTS**	
Jersey	*Caesarea*	Africa	*Libya, Africa*
Kent	*Cantium*	Europe	*Europa*
Lanchester	*Longovicium*		
Land's End	*Bolerium*	**COUNTRIES AND REGIONS**	
	Promunturium	Belgium	*Belgae*
Leicester	*Ratae*	Brittany	*Armoricae*
	Corieltauvorum	China	*Seres*

Denmark	*Dania*	Caspian Sea	*Mare Caspium*
Egypt	*Aegyptus*	Dardanelles	*Hellespontus*
Flanders	*Menapii*	Gibraltar, Straits of	*Fretum*
France	*Gallia*		*Gaditanum*
Germany	*Germania*	Marmora, Sea of	*Propontis*
Gibraltar	*Calpe*	Mediterranean	*Mare Internum*
Greece	*Graecia*	Nile, R.	*Nilus*
Holland	*Batavi*	Persian Gulf	*Sinus Arabicus*
Italy	*Italia*	Red Sea	*Mare Rubrim*
Lebanon	*Libanus*	Rhine, R.	*Rhenus*
Malta	*Melita*	Tyrrhenian Sea	*Mare Inferum*
Morocco	*Mauretania*		
Portugal	*Lusitania*	CITIES	
Spain	*Hispania*	Berlin	*Berolinum*
Switzerland	*Helvetia*	Bern	*Verona*
Tuscany	*Etruria*	Cadiz	*Gades*
		Istanbul	*Byzantium*
SEAS AND RIVERS		Jerusalem	*Hierosolyma*
Atlantic Ocean	*Mare Atlanticum*	Lisbon	*Olisipo*
Black Sea	*Pontus (Euxinus)*	Paris	*Lutetia*

GREEK AND ROMAN GODS

GREEK NAME	ROMAN NAME	SYMBOLISING
The Olympians	*Consentes Dii*	
Aphrodite	Venus	Beauty and love
Apollo	Apollo	Music, poetry and the Sun
Ares	Mars	War
Artemis	Diana	Hunting and animals
Athena	Minerva	Education and wisdom
Demeter	Ceres	The Earth and agriculture
Dionysus	Bacchus	Revelry, theatre and wine
Hades	Pluto	Death and the Underworld
Hebe	Juventas	Youth
Helios	Sol	The Sun
Hephaestus	Vulcan	Fire and crafts
Hera	Juno	Fidelity and marriage
Hermes	Mercury	Messenger of the gods
Hestia	Vesta	Family and the home
Persephone	Proserpine	Death and the Underworld
Poseidon	Neptune	The sea
Zeus	Jupiter	Ruler of the gods

The Olympians were the principal gods in Greek mythology (their Roman counterparts were known as the *Consentes Dii*) and lived at the top of Mount Olympus, the tallest peak in Greece. The previous occupants of Mount Olympus were the Titans, a powerful group of deities led by Cronus who ruled the Earth. The Olympians, led by Zeus, overthrew the Titans in the Titan War and imprisoned them in Tartarus in the Underworld.

There were never more than twelve Olympians at any one time, but the gods listed above have all been recognised as Olympians at some point.

ROYALTY

THE BRITISH ROYAL FAMILY

ORDER OF SUCCESSION TO THE THRONE

1   HRH The Prince of Wales
2   HRH Prince William of Wales
3   HRH Prince Henry of Wales
4   HRH The Duke of York
5   HRH Princess Beatrice of York
6   HRH Princess Eugenie of York
7   HRH The Earl of Wessex
8   HRH The Princess Royal
9   Peter Phillips
10 Zara Phillips
11 Viscount Linley
12 Hon. Charles Armstrong-Jones
13 Hon. Margarita Armstrong-Jones
14 Lady Sarah Chatto
15 Samuel Chatto
16 Arthur Chatto
17 HRH The Duke of Gloucester
18 Earl of Ulster
19 Lady Davina Lewis
20 Lord Culloden
21 Lady Rose Windsor
22 HRH The Duke of Kent
23 Baron Downpatrick
24 Lady Marina-Charlotte Windsor
25 Lady Amelia Windsor
26 Lady Helen Taylor
27 Columbus Taylor
28 Cassius Taylor
29 Eloise Taylor
30 Estella Taylor
31 Lord Frederick Windsor
32 Lady Gabriella Windsor
33 HRH Princess Alexandra, the Hon. Lady Ogilvy
34 James Ogilvy
35 Alexander Ogilvy
36 Flora Ogilvy
37 Marina Ogilvy, Mrs Mowatt
38 Christian Mowatt
39 Zenouska Mowatt

The Earl of St Andrews and HRH Prince Michael of Kent lost their right of succession to the throne through marriage to a Roman Catholic. Lord Nicholas Windsor and Baron Downpatrick renounced their rights to the throne on converting to Roman Catholicism in 2001 and 2003 respectively. Their children remain in succession provided that they are in communion with the Church of England.

KINGS AND QUEENS

ENGLISH KINGS AND QUEENS, 927 TO 1603

HOUSES OF CERDIC AND DENMARK

REIGN

927–39	Æthelstan (?–939)
939–46	Edmund I (921–46)
946–55	Eadred (?–955)
955–59	Eadwig (c.943–?)
959–75	Edgar I (943–75)
975–78	Edward I (the Martyr) (c.962–978)
978–1016	Æthelred (the Unready) (c.968/9–1016)
1016	Edmund II (Ironside) (before 993–1016)
1016–35	Cnut (Canute) (c.995–1035)
1035–40	Harold I (Harefoot) (c.1016/17–40)
1040–42	Harthacnut (Harthacanute) (c.1018–42)
1042–66	Edward II (the Confessor) (c.1002/5–66)
1066	Harold II (Godwinesson) (c.1020–66)

THE HOUSE OF NORMANDY

REIGN

1066–87	William I (the Conqueror) (c.1027–87)
1087–1100	William II (Rufus) (c.1056/60–1100)
1100–35	Henry I (Beauclerk) (1068–1135)
1135–54	Stephen (before 1100–54)

THE HOUSE OF ANJOU (PLANTAGENETS)

REIGN

1154–89	Henry II (Curtmantle) (1133–89)
1189–99	Richard I (Coeur de Lion) (1157–99)
1199–1216	John (Lackland) (1167–1216)
1216–72	Henry III (1207–72)
1272–1307	Edward I (Longshanks) (1239–1307)
1307–27	Edward II (1284–1327)
1327–77	Edward III (1312–77)
1377–99	Richard II (1367–1400)

THE HOUSE OF LANCASTER

REIGN	
1399–1413	Henry IV (1366–1413)
1413–22	Henry V (1387–1422)
1422–71	Henry VI (1421–71)

THE HOUSE OF YORK

REIGN	
1461–83	Edward IV (1442–83)
1483	Edward V (1470–83)
1483–85	Richard III (1452–85)

THE HOUSE OF TUDOR

REIGN	
1485–1509	Henry VII (1457–1509)
1509–47	Henry VIII (1491–1547)
1547–53	Edward VI (1537–53)
1553	Jane (1537–54)
1553–58	Mary I (1516–58)
1558–1603	Elizabeth I (1533–1603)

BRITISH KINGS AND QUEENS SINCE 1603
THE HOUSE OF STUART

REIGN	
1603–25	James I (VI of Scotland) (1566–1625)
1625–49	Charles I (1600–49)
	Commonwealth declared 19 May 1649
1649–53	Government by a council of state
1653–58	Oliver Cromwell, Lord Protector
1658–59	Richard Cromwell, Lord Protector
	Restoration of the monarchy
1660–85	Charles II (1630–85)
1685–88	James II (VII of Scotland) (1633–1701)
	Interregnum 11 December 1688 to 12 February 1689
1689–1702	William III (1650–1702)
1689–94	Mary II (1662–94)
1702–14	Anne (1665–1714)

THE HOUSE OF HANOVER

REIGN

1714–27	George I (Elector of Hanover) (1660–1727)
1727–60	George II (1683–1760)
1760–1820	George III (1738–1820)
	Regency 1811–20
	Prince of Wales regent owing to the insanity of George III
1820–30	George IV (1762–1830)
1830–37	William IV (1765–1837)
1837–1901	Victoria (1819–1901)

THE HOUSE OF SAXE-COBURG AND GOTHA

REIGN

1901–10	Edward VII (1841–1910)

THE HOUSE OF WINDSOR

REIGN

1910–36	George V (1865–1936)
1936	Edward VIII (1894–1972)
1936–52	George VI (1895–1952)
1952–	Elizabeth II (1926–)

KINGS AND QUEENS OF SCOTS, 1016 TO 1603

REIGN

1016–34	Malcolm II (c.954–1034)

THE HOUSE OF ATHOLL

REIGN

1034–40	Duncan I
1040–57	Macbeth (c.1005–57)
1057–58	Lulach (c.1032–58)
1058–93	Malcolm III (Canmore) (c.1031–93)
1093–97	Donald III Ban (c.1033–1100)
	Deposed May 1094, restored November 1094
1094	Duncan II (c.1060–94)
1097–1107	Edgar (c.1074–1107)
1107–24	Alexander I (The Fierce) (c.1077–1124)
1124–53	David I (The Saint) (c.1085–1153)
1153–65	Malcolm IV (The Maiden) (c.1141–65)
1165–1214	William I (The Lion) (c.1142–1214)
1214–49	Alexander II (1198–1249)

1249–86	Alexander III (1241–86)
1286–90	Margaret (The Maid of Norway) (1283–90)
	First Interregnum 1290–92
	Throne disputed by 13 competitors. Crown awarded to John Balliol by adjudication of Edward I of England

THE HOUSE OF BALLIOL
REIGN

1292–96	John (Balliol) (c.1250–1313)
	Second Interregnum 1296–1306
	Edward I of England declared John Balliol to have forfeited the throne for contumacy in 1296, and took the government of Scotland into his own hands

THE HOUSE OF BRUCE
REIGN

1306–29	Robert I (Bruce) (1274–1329)
1329–71	David II (1324–71)
	1332 Edward Balliol, son of John Balliol, crowned King of Scots September, expelled December
1333–36	Edward Balliol restored as King of Scots

THE HOUSE OF STEWART
REIGN

1371–90	Robert II (Stewart) (1316–90)
1390–1406	Robert III (c.1337–1406)
1406–37	James I (1394–1437)
1437–60	James II (1430–60)
1460–88	James III (1452–88)
1488–1513	James IV (1473–1513)
1513–42	James V (1512–42)
1542–67	Mary (1542–87)
1567–1625	James VI (and I of England) (1566–1625)
	Succeeded 1603 to the English throne, so joining the English and Scottish crowns

WELSH SOVEREIGNS AND PRINCES

Wales was ruled by sovereign princes from the earliest times until the death of Llywelyn in 1282. The first English Prince of Wales was the son of Edward I, who was born in Caernarvon town on 25 April 1284. According to a discredited legend, he was presented to the Welsh chieftains as their prince, in fulfilment of a promise that they should have a prince who 'could not speak a word of English' and should be native born. This son, who afterwards became Edward II, was created 'Prince of Wales and Earl of Chester' at the Lincoln Parliament on 7 February 1301.

The title Prince of Wales is borne after individual conferment and is not inherited at birth, though some princes have been declared and styled Prince of Wales but never formally so created (marked (s.) in the following lists). The title was conferred on Prince Charles by The Queen on 26 July 1958. He was invested at Caernarvon on 1 July 1969.

INDEPENDENT PRINCES, 844 TO 1282

REIGN

844–78	Rhodri the Great
878–916	Anarawd, son of Rhodri
916–50	Hywel Dda, the Good
950–79	Iago ab Idwal (or Ieuaf)
979–85	Hywel ab Ieuaf, the Bad
985–86	Cadwallon, his brother
986–99	Maredudd ab Owain ap Hywel Dda
999–1008	Cynan ap Hywel ab Ieuaf
1018–23	Llywelyn ap Seisyll
1023–39	Iago ab Idwal ap Meurig
1039–63	Gruffydd ap Llywelyn ap Seisyll
1063–75	Bleddyn ap Cynfyn
1075–81	Trahaern ap Caradog
1081–1137	Gruffydd ap Cynan ab Iago
1137–70	Owain Gwynedd
1170–94	Dafydd ab Owain Gwynedd
1194–1240	Llywelyn Fawr, the Great
1240–46	Dafydd ap Llywelyn
1246–82	Llywelyn ap Gruffydd ap Llywelyn

ENGLISH PRINCES SINCE 1301

1301	Edward (Edward II)
1343	Edward the Black Prince, son of Edward III
1376	Richard (Richard II), son of the Black Prince
1399	Henry of Monmouth (Henry V)
1454	Edward of Westminster, son of Henry VI
1471	Edward of Westminster (Edward V)
1483	Edward, son of Richard III (d. 1484)
1489	Arthur Tudor, son of Henry VII
1504	Henry Tudor (Henry VIII)
1610	Henry Stuart, son of James I (d. 1612)
1616	Charles Stuart (Charles I)
c.1638 (s.)	Charles Stuart (Charles II)
1688 (s.)	James Francis Edward Stuart (The Old Pretender), son of James II
1714	George Augustus (George II)
1729	Frederick Lewis, son of George II (d. 1751)
1751	George William Frederick (George III)
1762	George Augustus Frederick (George IV)
1841	Albert Edward (Edward VII)
1901	George (George V)
1910	Edward (Edward VIII)
1958	Charles, son of Elizabeth II

PRINCESSES ROYAL

The style Princess Royal is conferred at the Sovereign's discretion on his or her eldest daughter. It is an honorary title, held for life, and cannot be inherited or passed on. It was first conferred on Princess Mary, daughter of Charles I, in approximately 1642.

c.1642	Princess Mary (1631–60), daughter of Charles I
1727	Princess Anne (1709–59), daughter of George II
1766	Princess Charlotte (1766–1828), daughter of George III
1840	Princess Victoria (1840–1901), daughter of Victoria
1905	Princess Louise (1867–1931), daughter of Edward VII
1932	Princess Mary (1897–1965), daughter of George V
1987	Princess Anne (b. 1950), daughter of Elizabeth II

THE WIVES OF HENRY VIII

MARRIED	WIFE	ISSUE
1509–33	Catherine of Aragon (divorced)	Henry, Duke of Cornwall (b. & d. 1510) Mary I (1516–1558)*
1533–6	Anne Boleyn (beheaded)	Henry, Duke of Cornwall (b. & d. 1534) Elizabeth I (1533–1603)
1536–7	Jane Seymour (died)	Edward VI (1537–1553)
1540	Anne of Cleves (divorced)	–
1540–2	Catherine Howard (beheaded)	–
1543–7	Catherine Parr (survived)	–

* Catherine of Aragon gave birth to six children in total; two were born alive and only Mary I survived infancy

WORLD MONARCHIES

The following is a list of those countries of the world that are monarchies or principalities, showing the head of state and his/her date of accession to the throne.

Bahrain	Shaikh Hamad bin Isa al-Khalifa, acceded 7 March 1999
Belgium	King Albert II, acceded 9 August 1993
Bhutan	King Jigme Khesar Namgyel Wangchuk, acceded December 2006
Brunei	Sultan Hassanal Bolkiah, acceded 1967
Cambodia	King Norodom Sihamoni, acceded 14 October 2004
Denmark	Queen Margrethe II, acceded 14 January 1972
Japan	Emperor Akihito, acceded 8 January 1989
Jordan	King Abdullah II, acceded 7 February 1999
Kuwait	Shaikh Sabah al-Ahmed al-Jaber al-Sabah, sworn in 29 January 2006
Lesotho	King Letsie III, acceded February 1996
Liechtenstein	Prince Hans Adam II, acceded 13 November 1989
Luxembourg	Grand Duke Henri, acceded 7 October 2000
Malaysia	Sultan Mizan Zainal Abidin, sworn in 13 December 2006
Monaco	Prince Albert II, acceded 1 April 2005
Morocco	King Mohammed VI, acceded 23 July 1999
Nepal	King Gyanendra Bir Bikram Shah Dev, acceded 4 June 2001
The Netherlands	Queen Beatrix, acceded 30 April 1980
Norway	King Harald V, acceded 17 January 1991
Oman	Sultan Qaboos bin Said al-Said, acceded 23 July 1970

Qatar	Shaikh Hamad bin Khalifa al-Thani, assumed power 27 June 1995
Samoa	Susuga Malietoa Tanumafili II, acceded 15 April 1963
Saudi Arabia	King Abdullah Bin-Abd-al-Aziz Al Saud, acceded 1 August 2005
Spain	King Juan Carlos I, acceded 22 November 1975
Swaziland	King Mswati III, acceded 25 April 1986
Sweden	King Carl XVI Gustaf, acceded 15 September 1973
Thailand	King Bhumibol Adulyadej, acceded 9 June 1946
Tonga	King George Tupou V, acceded 11 September 2006
United Kingdom	Queen Elizabeth II*, acceded 6 February 1952

* Also head of state in Antigua and Barbuda, Australia, The Bahamas, Barbados, Belize, Canada, Grenada, Jamaica, New Zealand, Papua New Guinea, St Christopher and Nevis, St Lucia, St Vincent and the Grenadines, Solomon Islands and Tuvalu

SCIENCE

THE SOLAR SYSTEM

	MEAN DISTANCE FROM SUN KM 10^6	PERIOD OF ROTATION ON AXIS DAYS	DIAMETER KM
Sun	—	25–35*	

PLANETS†

Mercury	58	58.646	4,878
Venus	108	243.019r	12,100
Earth	150	0.997	12,756
Mars	228	1.026	6,794
Jupiter	778	0.410e	142,800
Saturn	1,427	0.426e	120,000
Uranus	2,870	0.718r	52,400
Neptune	4,497	0.671	48,400

* depending on latitude, r retrograde, e equatorial

† In August 2006 Pluto was reclassified by the International Astronomical Union as a dwarf planet

SATELLITES OF THE PLANETS

	MEAN DISTANCE FROM PLANET KM	PERIOD OF REVOLUTION ROUND PLANET DAYS
EARTH		
Moon	384,400	27.322
MARS		
Phobos	9,378	0.319
Deimos	23,459	1.262
JUPITER		
Metis	127,960	0.295
Adrastea	128,980	0.298
Amalthea	181,300	0.498
Thebe	221,900	0.675
Io	421,600	1.769
Europa	670,900	3.551
Ganymede	1,070,000	7.155
Callisto	1,883,000	16.689
Leda	11,094,000	239.000
Himalia	11,480,000	251.000
Lysithea	11,720,000	259
Elara	11,737,000	260
Ananke	21,200,000	631r
Carme	22,600,000	692r
Pasiphae	23,500,000	735r
Sinope	23,700,000	758r
SATURN		
Pan	133,583	0.575
Atlas	137,670	0.602
Prometheus	139,353	0.613
Pandora	141,700	0.629
Epimetheus	151,422	0.694
Janus	151,472	0.695
Mimas	185,520	0.942
Enceladus	238,020	1.370
Tethys	294,660	1.888

Telesto	294,660	1.888
Calypso	294,660	1.888
Dione	377,400	2.737
Helene	377,400	2.737
Rhea	527,040	4.518
Titan	1,221,830	15.945
Hyperion	1,481,100	21.277
Iapetus	3,561,300	79.330
Phoebe	12,952,000	550.48r

URANUS		
Cordelia	49,770	0.335
Ophelia	53,790	0.376
Bianca	59,170	0.435
Cressida	61,780	0.464
Desdemona	62,680	0.474
Juliet	64,350	0.493
Portia	66,090	0.513
Rosalind	69,940	0.558
Belinda	75,260	0.624
Puck	86,010	0.762

Miranda	129,390	1.413
Ariel	191,020	2.520
Umbriel	266,300	4.144
Titania	435,910	8.706
Oberon	583,520	13.463
S/1997 U1	72,000,000	579
S/1997 U2	122,000,000	1,289

NEPTUNE		
Naiad	48,230	0.294
Thalassa	50,070	0.311
Despina	52,530	0.335
Galatea	61,950	0.429
Larissa	73,550	0.555
Proteus	117,650	1.122
Triton	354,760	5.877
Nereid	5,513,400	360.136

DWARF PLANETS

Ceres, Eris, Pluto

r retrograde

SI UNITS

The Système International d'Unités (SI) is an international and coherent system of units devised to meet all known needs for measurement in science and technology; it was adopted in 1960.

The system consists of seven base units and the derived units formed as products or quotients of various powers of the base units.

BASE UNITS

metre (m)	= unit of length
kilogram (kg)	= unit of mass
second (s)	= unit of time
ampere (A)	= unit of electric current
kelvin (K)	= unit of thermodynamic temperature
mole (mol)	= unit of amount of substance
candela (cd)	= unit of luminous intensity

DERIVED UNITS

hertz (Hz)	= unit of frequency
newton (N)	= unit of force
pascal (Pa)	= unit of pressure, stress
joule (J)	= unit of energy, work, quantity of heat
watt (W)	= unit of power, radiant flux
coulomb (C)	= unit of electric charge, quantity of electricity
volt (V)	= unit of electric potential, potential difference, electromotive force
farad (F)	= unit of electric capacitance
ohm (Ω)	= unit of electric resistance
siemens (S)	= unit of electric conductance
weber (Wb)	= unit of magnetic flux
tesla (T)	= unit of magnetic flux density
henry (H)	= unit of inductance degree
Celsius (°C)	= unit of Celsius temperature
lumen (lm)	= unit of luminous flux
lux (lx)	= unit of illuminance
becquerel (Bq)	= unit of activity (of a radionuclide)
gray (Gy)	= unit of absorbed dose, specific energy imparted, kerma, absorbed dose index
sievert (Sv)	= unit of dose equivalent, dose equivalent index
radian (rad)	= unit of plane angle
steradian (sr)	= unit of solid angle

OTHER DERIVED UNITS

Other derived units are expressed in terms of base units. Some of the more commonly used are:

Unit of area	= square metre (m^2)
Unit of volume	= cubic metre (m^3)
Unit of velocity	= metre per second ($m\ s^{-1}$)
Unit of acceleration	= metre per second squared ($m\ s^{-2}$)
Unit of density	= kilogram per cubic metre ($kg\ m^{-3}$)
Unit of momentum	= kilogram metre per second ($kg\ m\ s^{-1}$)
Unit of magnetic field strength	= ampere per metre ($A\ m^{-1}$)
Unit of surface tension	= newton per metre ($N\ m^{-1}$)
Unit of dynamic viscosity	= pascal second ($Pa\ s$)
Unit of heat capacity	= joule per kelvin ($J\ K^{-1}$)
Unit of specific heat capacity	= joule per kilogram kelvin ($J\ kg^{-1}\ K^{-1}$)
Unit of heat flux density, irradiance	= watt per square metre ($W\ m^{-1}$)
Unit of thermal conductivity	= watt per metre kelvin ($W\ m^{-1}\ K^{-1}$)

Unit of electric field strength   = volt per metre (V m^{-1})
Unit of luminance   = candela per square metre (cd m^{-2})

SI PREFIXES

Decimal multiples and submultiples of the SI units are indicated by SI prefixes. These are as follows:

MULTIPLES
yotta (Y) x 10^{24}
zetta (Z) x 10^{21}
exa (E) x 10^{18}
peta (P) x 10^{15}
tera (T) x 10^{12}
giga (G) x 10^9
mega (M) x 10^6
kilo (k) x 10^3
hecto (h) x 10^2
deca (da) x 10

SUBMULTIPLES
deci (d) x 10^{-1}
centi (c) x 10^{-2}
milli (m) x 10^{-3}
micro (i) x 10^{-6}
nano (n) x 10^{-9}
pico (p) x 10^{-12}
femto (f) x 10^{-15}
atto (a) x 10^{-18}
zepto (z) x 10^{-21}
yocto (y) x 10^{-24}

SOME SI UNIT DEFINITIONS

1 metre is the distance travelled by light in a vacuum in one 299,792,458th of a second

1 kilogram is a cylinder of platinum-iridium alloy held by the International Bureau of Weights and Measures at Sevres, near Paris (the only remaining artifact-based standard measure in use)

1 second is 9,192,631,770 radiation cycles of the cesium-133 atom

1 ampere is the magnitude of a current that results in a force equal to 2×10^7

1 kelvin is the point immediately above absolute zero, where all atomic activity ceases

1 mole is the amount of a substance that contains as many elementary entities as there are atoms in 12 grams of carbon-12

PHYSICS

DEFINITIONS AND LAWS

Acceleration (symbol: *a*): the rate of change of velocity (a vector quantity). SI unit: metre per second squared.

$$\frac{\text{change in velocity}}{\text{time taken for this change}} \qquad \text{metres/second}^2 \text{ (m s}^{-2})$$

Archimedes' principle (Greek mathematician, 287–212 BC): a body that is partially or totally immersed in a fluid is buoyed up by a force that is equal to the weight of the fluid displaced by the body.

Density (symbol: ρ): mass divided by volume (a physical quantity). SI unit: kilogram per cubic metre.

Energy (symbol: *E*): the capacity of a body or system to do work (a physical quantity). SI unit: joule.

Force (symbol *F*): that which causes a body to change its state at rest or linear motion (a vector quantity). The magnitude of the force is equal to the product *ma* where
    m = mass of the body.
    a = acceleration imparted by the force.

Gravitation (Newton's law of): the force of attraction between two given bodies in the universe is directly proportional to the product of their masses and inversely proportional to the square of the distance between them.

Inertia: see Newton's first law of motion.

Mass (symbol: *m*): measures a body's inertia and determines the mutual gravitational attraction between it and another body. SI unit: kilogram. Mass is the amount of 'stuff' in the body. Mass does not depend on gravitational attraction.

Momentum (symbol: *p*): the product of mass and velocity (a physical and vector quantity). SI unit: kilogram metre per second.

Newton's laws of motion (Sir Isaac Newton, 1642–1727)
1   A body will remain in a state of rest or travel in a straight line at constant speed unless acted upon by an external force, e.g. inertia.

2   The rate of change of momentum of a moving body is proportional to and in the same direction as the force acting on it.

3   To every action there is always an equal and opposite reaction.

Power (symbol *P*): the rate of doing work or of heat transfer (a physical quantity). SI unit: watt (1 watt = 1 joule per second).

$$\text{average power} = \frac{\text{work done}}{\text{time taken}} = \frac{\text{energy change}}{\text{time taken}}$$

Pressure (symbol: *p*): the force acting per unit surface area, expressed as

$$\text{pressure} = \frac{\text{force}}{\text{area}}$$

SI unit: pascal (Pa).

Atmospheric pressure is still quoted in millibars. The standard atmospheric pressure at 1013 millibars (Mb) is 1 kilogram cm^{-2}.
NB: tyre pressures are still quoted in lb/sq.in. or, more recently, Bar, e.g. 2 Bar.

Relativity, theory of: mass and energy are related by the equation $E = mc^2$, where E is the energy produced by a mass change m, and c is the speed of light.

Scalar: a physical quantity that has magnitude but not direction, e.g. mass (see also vector).

Speed (symbol: *v* or *u*): the rate of change of distance travelled (a scalar quantity). SI unit: metre per second.

$$\text{average speed} = \frac{\text{distance moved}}{\text{time taken}} \qquad \text{m s}^{-1}$$

Time (symbol: *t*): a fundamental physical quantity indicating duration or precise moment. SI unit: second.

Vector: a physical quantity that has magnitude and direction, e.g. acceleration.

Velocity (symbol *v* or *c*): the rate of change of displacement (a vector quantity). SI unit: metre per second.

$$\text{average velocity} = \frac{\text{distance moved in a particular direction}}{\text{time taken}} \qquad \text{m s}^{-1}$$

Weight (symbol: W): the gravitational force exerted on a body at a planet's surface, giving it an acceleration equal to the acceleration of free fall, g. It should not be confused with mass *(m)*: $W = mg$, and therefore varies as g varies. (SI unit: newton, although it is measured in units of mass in everyday usage.)

Work (symbol: W): a physical quantity expressed as force x distance (Fs) where the point of application of a force moves through a distance in the direction of the force. SI unit: joule.

CONSTANTS
GRAVITY
Acceleration of gravity (standard value of acceleration of free fall) (symbol: g_n): 9.806 65 m s^{-2}. The acceleration of gravity varies in different places on the Earth's surface. At Greenwich: 9.81 ms^{-2}.

Gravitational constant (symbol: G): 6.672 59 x 10^{-11} N m^2 kg^{-2}.

LIGHT
Speed of light in a vacuum (symbol: c): 299 792 458 m s^{-1}.

SOUND
Speed of sound (symbol: c): 331.4 m s^{-1} (in dry air at 0°C).

WAVES
A wave is a periodic vibration in space or in a substance. Waves can be grouped in two ways according to:
1) whether or not they result in a transfer of energy from one place to another:
Travelling (or progressive) wave: the vibrations travel, transferring energy from one place to another, e.g. the waves on the sea
Stationary (or standing) wave: the wave shape remains stationary, rather than moving, and energy is not transferred
2) whether or not the individual points on the wave move in the same direction as the wave itself:
Longitudinal wave: particles move in the same direction as the wave travels, e.g. in a slinky spring
Transverse wave: particles move in a perpendicular direction to the direction of wave travel, e.g. in water waves

PROPERTIES OF WAVES
Amplitude

Amplitude is the maximum displacement of a wave from the equilibrium position

Wavelength

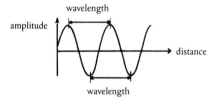

Wavelength is the distance between two successive points along a wave with similar amplitudes

Period

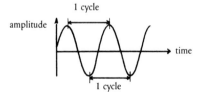

The period of a wave is the time taken for one complete cycle.
Frequency = cycles per second. SI unit: hertz (Hz).
1 cycle per second = 1 hertz

Wave Attenuation

 distance

A wave is said to be attenuated when its amplitude becomes progressively reduced as a result of energy loss when it travels through a medium.

SOUND

Decibels (db) are used to measure the power or intensity of sound. Some examples of decibel levels are:

Silence	0db
Noise level of ordinary conversation	60db
Damage threshold for noise	90db
Noise level of typical streetworks	110db
Pain threshold for noise	130db

CHEMISTRY

STATES OF MATTER

The three states of matter are: solid, liquid and gas. When heated, a solid melts to form a liquid. Melting (or freezing) point is the temperature above which a solid becomes a liquid. Heating a liquid to its boiling point causes it to boil and form a gas or vapour.

PROPERTY	SOLID	LIQUID	GAS
Volume	Definite	Definite	Variable – expands or contracts to fill container
Shape	Definite	Takes up shape of bottom of container	Takes up shape of whole container
Density	High	Medium	Low
Expansion when heated	Low	Medium	High
Effect of applied pressure	Very slight	Slight decrease in volume	Large decrease in volume
Movement of particles	Very slow	Medium	Fast

ELEMENTS AND COMPOUNDS

ELEMENTS

An element is a pure substance that cannot be split up by chemical reaction. There are 92 known to occur naturally on Earth, and more which have been synthesised under laboratory conditions. Most that occur naturally are solid and metallic at room temperature and pressure, although there are exceptions, e.g. mercury is a liquid and oxygen is a gas.

COMPOUNDS

Some mixtures of elements react together, usually when heated, to form compounds. These compounds have very different properties from the elements of which they are composed, e.g. the gases hydrogen and oxygen combine to form water (H_2O).

NAMING COMPOUNDS

Compounds with the prefix **per-** contain extra oxygen

Compounds with the prefix **thio-** contain a sulphur atom in place of an oxygen atom

Compounds that end in **-ide** contain two elements

Compounds that end in **-ate** or **-ite** contain oxygen

FORMULAE OF SOME COMMON COMPOUNDS

COMPOUND	FORMULA
Ammonia	NH_3
Carbon dioxide	CO_2
Carbon monoxide	CO
Hydrogen chloride	HCl
Methane	CH_4
Nitrogen dioxide	NO_2
Sulphur dioxide	SO_2
Sulphur trioxide	SO_3
Water	H_2O
Table salt	$NaCl$

CARBON

Carbon can combine with other elements, notably oxygen, nitrogen and hydrogen, to form the large molecules of which living things are made, e.g., carbohydrates, fats and proteins.

METALS AND ALLOYS

Metals consist of a close-packed, regular arrangement of positive ions surrounded by electrons that hold the ions together (see Atomic Structure). With a few exceptions, they are efficient conductors of heat and electricity, and are both malleable (can be beaten into thin sheets) and ductile (can be extruded into wire). Metals are often combined to form alloys, common examples including:

ALLOY	CONSTITUENT ELEMENTS
Brass	Copper and zinc
Bronze	Copper and tin
Duralumin	Aluminium, magnesium, copper and manganese
Solder	Tin and lead
Steel	Iron and carbon, although other metals may be present, e.g. chromium

ATOMIC STRUCTURE

All elements are made up of atoms. An atom is the smallest unit of an element, and atoms of different elements are made up of different combinations of three basic particles: protons, electrons and neutrons. Protons have a positive charge, electrons have a negative charge and neutrons have no charge.

In an atom, the protons and neutrons are tightly packed in the nucleus, while the electrons move rapidly around the outside. The atomic number of an atom is the number of protons it contains, and the mass number is the total number of protons and neutrons.

Atoms contain the same number of protons as electrons, which means that individual atoms have no overall charge. However, an ion is an electrically charged atom or group of atoms formed by the addition or loss of one or more electrons.

ATOMIC BONDING

When atoms join they are said to bond. Several types of bonding occur in common chemicals.

Ionic (or electrovalent) bonding: involves a complete transfer of electrons from one atom to another.

Covalent bonding: involves the sharing of electrons rather than complete transfer.

Metallic bonding: occurs only in metals.

CHEMICAL GROUPS

Elements can be divided into groups, which include the following.

THE ALKALI METAL GROUP
This is a group of very reactive metals, the most common of which are Lithium (Li), Sodium (Na) and Potassium (K).

THE HALOGEN GROUP
This is a group of non-metals, all of which are different in appearance but have similar chemical reactions. They include: Fluorine (F), Chlorine (Cl), Bromine (Br) and Iodine (I).

THE NOBLE (OR INERT) GAS GROUP
As their name suggests, these gases are unreactive:

Helium (He)
Neon (Ne)
Argon (Ar)
Krypton (Kr)
Xenon (Xe)
Radon (Rn)

MELTING AND BOILING POINTS OF SELECTED COMPOUNDS AND ELEMENTS

COMPOUND	MELTING POINT (°C)	BOILING POINT (°C)
Ammonia (NH_3)	−77.7	−33.3
Carbon dioxide (CO_2)	−56.6	−78.5
Ethyl alcohol (C_2H_5OH)	−114.1	78.5
Hydrogen chloride (HCl)	−114.0	−85.0
Hydrogen peroxide (H_2O_2)	−0.4	150.2
Methane (CH_4)	−182.5	−162.0
Ozone (O_3)	−251.4	−112.0
Propane (C_3H_8)	−187.6	−42.1
Sulphuric acid (H_2SO_4)	10.4	338.0
Water (H_2O)	0.0	100.0

ELEMENT	MELTING POINT (°C)	BOILING POINT (°C)
Aluminium (Al)	660.3	2,519.0
Argon (Ar)	−189.6	−185.9
Arsenic (As)	817.0	614.0
Cadmium (Cd)	321.1	767.0
Calcium (Ca)	842.0	1,484.0
Carbon (C)	4,492.0	3.6
Chlorine (Cl)	−101.5	34.0
Copper (Cu)	1,084.6	2,562.0
Gold (Au)	1,064.2	2,856.0
Hydrogen (H)	−259.3	−252.9
Iodine (I)	113.7	184.4
Iron (Fe)	1,538.0	2,861.0
Lead (Pb)	327.5	1,749.0
Lithium (Li)	180.5	1,342.0
Magnesium (Mg)	650.0	1,090.0
Manganese (Mn)	1,246.0	2,061.0
Mercury (Hg)	−38.8	356.7
Neon (Ne)	−248.6	−246.1
Nickel (Ni)	1,455.0	2,913.0
Nitrogen (N)	−210.0	−195.8
Oxygen (O)	−218.8	−183.0
Phosphorus (P)	44.2	280.5
Platinum (Pt)	1,768.4	3,825.0
Potassium (K)	63.4	759.0
Silver (Ag)	691.8	2,162.0

ELEMENT	MELTING POINT (° C)	BOILING POINT (° C)
Sodium (Na)	97.8	883.0
Sulphur (S)	115.2	444.6
Tin (Sn)	231.9	2,602.0
Uranium (U)	1,135.0	4,131.0
Xenon (Xe)	−111.8	−108.0
Zinc (Zn)	419.5	907.0

THE PH SCALE

The pH of a substance is a measure of its alkalinity or acidity. A pH reading below 7 indicates an acid solution while readings above 7 indicate an alkaline solution.

0	
1	
2	
3	Acid
4	
5	
6	
7	Neutral
8	
9	
10	
11	Alkaline
12	
13	
14	

Litmus paper shows whether a solution is acidic or alkaline: blue indicates an alkali and red an acid. It is possible to obtain special paper that gives an approximate measure of pH by colour change. For very accurate measurements a pH meter must be used.

APPROX. PH VALUES OF BODY FLUIDS

Blood	7.4–7.5
Saliva	6.4–7.4
Urine	5.7
Sweat	4–6.8
Breast milk	7.0
Semen	7.2
Stomach contents varies but approx.	2

CIRCULATION OF MATERIALS

There is a constant interchange between the materials of living things and the environment, e.g. the air, soil and sea. Plants absorb carbon dioxide (CO_2) from the air for photosynthesis to make carbohydrates. Plants and animals release CO_2 when they respire. Oxygen is released by plants during photosynthesis and used by nearly all organisms for respiration.

Simple nitrogen compounds (e.g. nitrates) are absorbed by plant roots and used to build proteins. This nitrogen returns to the soil when living things die and decay. The supply of available nitrogen is also increased by nitrogen-fixing soil bacteria and lightning.

Most water absorbed from the soil passes straight through the plant and evaporates (transpiration); some is retained for photosynthesis but eventually returned via respiration. This balance can be upset by man's activities such as excessive deforestation and the burning of fossil fuels.

THE PERIODIC TABLE

	Alkali metals I A	Alkaline earth metals II A				Transition metals			
			III B	IV B	V B	VI B	V II		VIII
1	1 Hydrogen **H** 1.01								
2	3 Lithium **Li** 6.94	4 Beryllium **Be** 9.01							
3	11 Sodium **Na** 22.99	12 Magnesium **Mg** 24.31							
4	19 Potassium **K** 39.10	20 Calcium **Ca** 40.08	21 Scandium **Sc** 44.96	22 Titanium **Ti** 47.88	23 Vanadium **V** 50.94	24 Chromium **Cr** 52.00	25 Manganese **Mn** 54.95	26 Iron **Fe** 55.85	27 Coba **Co** 58.9
5	37 Rubidium **Rb** 85.47	38 Strontium **Sr** 87.62	39 Yttrium **Y** 88.91	40 Zirconium **Zr** 91.22	41 Niobium **Nb** 92.91	42 Molybdenum **Mo** 95.94	43 Technetium **Tc** 97.91	44 Ruthenium **Ru** 101.07	45 Rhodi **Rh** 102.
6	55 Caesium **Cs** 132.91	56 Barium **Ba** 137.33	Lanthanide series (see below)	72 Hafnium **Hf** 178.49	73 Tantalum **Ta** 180.94	74 Tungsten **W** 183.85	75 Rhenium **Ru** 186.21	76 Osmium **Os** 190.23	77 Iridiu **Ir** 192.
7	87 Francium **Fr** 223.02	88 Radium **Ra** 226.03	Actinide series (see below)	104 Rutherfordium **Rf** 261.12	105 Dubnium **Db** 262.11	106 Seaborgium **Sg** 236.12	107 Bohrium **Bh** 262	108 Hassium **Hs** 265	109 Meitner **M** 26

Rare earth elements—Lanthanide series	57 Lanthanum **La** 138.91	58 Cerium **Ce** 140.12	59 Praseodymium **Pr** 140.91	60 Neodymium **Nd** 144.24	61 Promethium **Pm** 144.91	62 Samar **Sn** 150.

Actinide series	89 Actinium **Ac** 227.03	90 Thorium **Th** 232.04	91 Protactinium **Pa** 231.04	92 Uranium **U** 238.03	93 Neptunium **Np** 237.05	94 Plutor **P** 244.

The Periodic Table arranges the elements into horizontal rows (periods) and vertical columns (groups) according to their at the left and electronegative to the right. The earliest version of the periodic table was devised in 1869 by Dmitriy Mendele

Noble
gases

								2 Helium **He** 4.00
			III A	IV A	V A	VI A	VII A	
			5 Boron **B** 10.81	6 Carbon **C** 12.01	7 Nitrogen **N** 14.01	8 Oxygen **O** 16.00	9 Fluorine **F** 19.00	10 Neon **Ne** 20.18

|---|---|---|---|---|---|---|---|---|
	I B	II B	13 Aluminium **Al** 26.98	14 Silicon **Si** 28.09	15 Phosphorus **P** 30.97	16 Sulphur **S** 32.07	17 Chlorine **Cl** 35.45	18 Argon **Ar** 39.95
28 Nickel **Ni** 58.70	29 Copper **Cu** 63.55	30 Zinc **Zn** 65.39	31 Gallium **Ga** 69.72	32 Germanium **Ge** 72.61	33 Arsenic **As** 74.92	34 Selenium **Se** 78.96	35 Bromine **Br** 79.904	36 Krypton **Kr** 83.80
46 Palladium **Pd** 106.4	47 Silver **Ag** 107.87	48 Cadmium **Cd** 112.41	49 Indium **In** 114.82	50 Tin **Sn** 118.71	51 Antimony **Sb** 121.74	52 Tellurium **Te** 127.60	53 Iodine **I** 126.9045	54 Xenon **Xe** 131.29
78 Platinum **Pt** 195.08	79 Gold **Au** 196.97	80 Mercury **Hg** 200.59	81 Thallium **Tl** 204.38	82 Lead **Pb** 207.2	83 Bismuth **Bi** 208.98	84 Polonium **Po** 209	85 Astatine **At** 210	86 Radon **Rn** 222.02
110 Darmstadtium **Ds** 269	111 Roentgenium **Rg** 272							

Non-metals

63 Europium **Eu** 151.96	64 Gadolinium **Gd** 157.25	65 Terbium **Tb** 158.93	66 Dysprosium **Dy** 162.50	67 Holmium **Ho** 164.93	68 Erbium **Er** 167.26	69 Thulium **Tm** 168.93	70 Ytterbium **Yb** 173.04	71 Lutetium **Lu** 174.97
95 Americium **Am** 243.06	96 Curium **Cm** 247.07	97 Berkelium **Bk** 247	98 Californium **Cf** 251.08	99 Einsteinium **Es** 252.08	100 Fermium **Fm** 257.10	101 Mendelevium **Md** 258.10	102 Nobelium **No** 259.10	103 Lawrencium **Lr** 260.11

...ber. The elements in a group all have similar properties; across each period, atoms are electropositive (form positive ions) to
...predicted the existence of several elements from gaps in the table.

THE STUDY OF . . .

Air in motion	Aerodynamics
Aircraft	Aeronautics
Animals	Zoology
Birds	Ornithology
Caves	Speleology
Cells	Cytology
Earthquakes	Seismology
Environment	Ecology
Fish	Ichthyology
Fluids	Hydraulics
Fossils and plants	Palaeontology
Fruit growing	Pomology
Fungi	Mycology
Handwriting	Graphology
Hormones	Endocrinology
Knowledge	Epistemology
Light	Optics
Low temperatures	Cryogenics
Maps	Cartography
Medicines	Pharmacology
Plants	Botany
Projectile motion	Ballistics
Reptiles	Herpetology
Rocks	Petrology
Skull	Phrenology
Speech patterns	Phonetics
Tissues of organisms	Histology
Trees	Dendrology
Tree rings	Dendrochronology
Universe	Cosmology
Words (history)	Etymology
Words (meaning)	Semantics

SCIENTIFIC INSTRUMENTS AND THEIR USES

Altimeter	Altitude
Ammeter	Electric current
Anemometer	Wind speed
Barometer	Atmospheric pressure
Calorimeter	Heat energy
Chronometer	Time
Clinometer	Angle of elevation
Craniometer	Skull size
Dynamometer	Engine power
Endoscope	Examining inside the body
Extensometer	Ductility
Gravimeter	Gravity
Hydrometer	Density of liquid
Hygrometer	Humidity
Lactometer	Density of milk
Manometer	Pressure
Micrometer	Small distances
Microscope	Magnification (of small objects)
Odometer	Distance
Pyrometer	High temperatures
Seismometer	Earthquakes
Sextant	Latitude
Spectroscope	Analysing light
Speedometer	Speed
Sphygmomanometer	Blood pressure
Tachometer	Rotational speed
Telescope	Magnification (of distant objects)
Thermometer	Temperature
Voltmeter	Voltage

LIFE SCIENCES

GENETICS AND EVOLUTION

Most cells have a nucleus containing a fixed number of chromosomes, half derived from each parent. The chromosomes carry genetic (inherited) information along their lengths as genes. In sexual reproduction the parents' genes are mixed and recombined so the offspring usually show characteristics of both.

In 1953, Crick and Watson in Cambridge showed that the genes were short lengths of deoxyribonucleic acid (DNA) and that the genetic information is contained in just four chemical groups taken three at a time. A gene is a sequence of these chemical 'words'. DNA is now used in the identification of individuals.

Charles Darwin (1809–82) described how the enormous variety of living things could have evolved through the 'natural selection' by the environment of those plants and animals best fitted to survive and reproduce themselves in the harshly competitive natural world.

CLASSIFICATION OF PLANTS AND ANIMALS

All species of plants and animals are named according to their genus and their species.

Species: the fundamental unit of biological classification; a group of organisms capable of breeding to produce fertile offspring. They are very similar, but do show variety. *Genus:* a category of biological classification; a group of organisms with a large number of similarities but whose different sub-groups or species are usually unable to interbreed successfully.

All species are named according to the binomial system invented by Carl Linnaeus in 1735. Under this system the genus name is written first, with a capital letter, e.g. *Homo* (man). The species name, which starts with a small letter, is written second, e.g. *sapiens* (modern).

GROUPS AND SUB-GROUPS

Just as species are sub-groups of genera, so Linnaeus grouped genera into larger and larger groups. They are listed as follows, from the largest (kingdom) to smallest (species):

Kingdom
Phylum (for animals) or
    Divisions (for plants)
Class
Order
Family
Genus
Species

The Plant Kingdom

The plant kingdom is divided into the following divisions, some of which are further sub-divided into two or more classes:

DIVISION	CLASS
Algae	
Bacteria	
Bryophyta	{ Musci (mosses) { Hepaticae (liverworts)
Fungi	
Lichens	
Pteridophyta	(Pteropsida (ferns) { Sphenopsida (horsetails) (Lycopsida (club-mosses)
Spermatophyta (seed-bearing plants)	{ Gymnosperms (cone-bearing) (Angiosperms (flower-bearing, seeds within fruits)

The Animal Kingdom
Invertebrates (no backbones)

PHYLUM	CLASS
Annelida (segmented worms)	
Arthropoda	(Arachnida (spiders) { Crustacea (hard outer shells) { Insecta (with a head, thorax and abdomen and 3 pairs of legs) (Myriapoda (with many legs)
Coelenterata (sac-like body, special sting cells)	
Echinodermata (symmetrical marine animals)	
Mollusca (shell, soft body)	
Nematoda (unsegmented worms)	
Platyhelminthes (flat-bodied worms)	
Protozoa (single-celled)	

Vertebrates (with backbones)

PHYLUM	CLASS
	Amphibia (living on land and water, can breathe dissolved or atmospheric oxygen)
	Aves (birds, feathered, constant body temperature)
Chordata	Mammalia (suckle their young, constant body temperature)
	Pisces (fish, breathe dissolved oxygen)
	Reptilia (scaly, cold-blooded, egg-laying)

PARTS OF A FLOWER

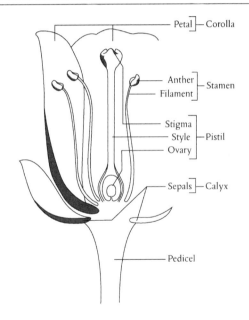

COLOURS OF THE RAINBOW

Red, orange, yellow, green, blue, indigo and violet

THE HUMAN BODY

THE SKELETON – FRONT VIEW

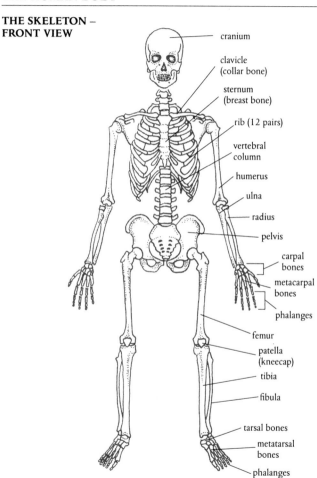

cranium

clavicle (collar bone)

sternum (breast bone)

rib (12 pairs)

vertebral column

humerus

ulna

radius

pelvis

carpal bones

metacarpal bones

phalanges

femur

patella (kneecap)

tibia

fibula

tarsal bones

metatarsal bones

phalanges

THE SKELETON –
SIDE VIEW

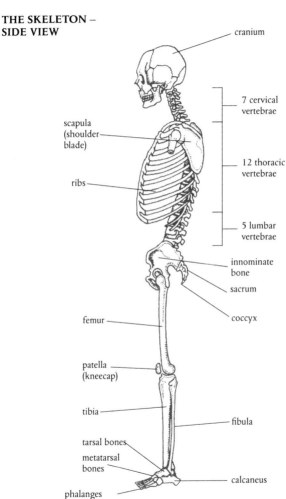

cranium

7 cervical vertebrae

scapula (shoulder blade)

12 thoracic vertebrae

ribs

5 lumbar vertebrae

innominate bone

sacrum

coccyx

femur

patella (kneecap)

tibia

fibula

tarsal bones

metatarsal bones

calcaneus

phalanges

MAIN MUSCLE GROUPS

MUSCLE GROUP	BODY PART	PRIMARY FUNCTIONS
abductors (gluteus medius and minimus)	outer thigh	draw hip outwards
adductors	inner thigh	draw hip inwards
anterior tibialis	shin	draws ball of the foot upwards
biceps brachii	upper arm, front	bends elbow
		swings shoulder joint forward
biceps femoris (hamstrings)	back of thigh	straightens hip
		bends knee and rotates it outwards
deltoideus	shoulder/upper arm	involved in all movements of upper arm
erector spinae	lower back	straightens spine
gastrocnemius	calf	bends knee
		straightens ankle (points toes)
gluteus maximus	buttocks	straightens hip
		rotates thigh outwards
iliopsoas (psoas major, iliacus)	hip	bends hip
		rotates leg outwards
latissimus dorsi (broad back muscle)	back	draws arm backwards
obliques (internal and external)	waist	rotate torso
		bend torso to side
pectoralis major (greater chest muscle)	chest	draws arm inwards
		pulls arm in front of chest from any position
quadriceps femoris (rectus femoris, vastus medialis, intermedialis, lateralis)	thigh	straightens knee
		bends hip
rectus abdominus	stomach	bends spine forwards
sartorius (tailor's muscle)	thigh	bends and rotates hip outwards
		bends and rotates knee inwards
soleus (flounder muscle)	lower calf	standing on toes
trapezius	neck and upper back	draws shoulder blades back
		turns head
		bends neck backwards
triceps brachii	upper arm, back	straightens elbow

PERIODS OF GESTATION OR INCUBATION

This table shows approximate periods of gestation or incubation for some common animals and birds; in some cases the periods may vary.

SPECIES	SHORTEST PERIOD (DAYS)	USUAL PERIOD (DAYS)	LONGEST PERIOD (DAYS)
Camel		45 weeks	
Canary	12	14	14
Cat	53	56	63
Chicken	20	21	22
Chimpanzee	216	237	261
Cow	273	280	294
Coyote	60	63	65
Dog	55	63	70
Duck	28	28	32
Elephant		21–22 months	
Fox	49	52	55
Goat	147	151	155
Giraffe	395	410	425
Goose	28	30	32
Guinea Pig	63	—	70
Hedgehog	35	38	40
Horse	305	336	340
Human	240	273	313
Mouse	18	—	19
Orangutan	245	260	275
Pig	109	112	125
Pigeon	17	18	19
Rabbit	30	32	35
Reindeer	215	230	245
Rat	21	—	24
Sheep	140	148	160
Tiger	105	107	109
Turkey	25	28	28
Zebra		56 weeks	

BRAIN AND BODY WEIGHTS OF ANIMALS

ANIMAL	BRAIN WEIGHT (G)	BODY WEIGHT (KG)
Cat	30	3
Chimpanzee	440	52
Cow	423	465
Dog (beagle)	72	14
Horse	655	521
Human	1,300	68
Pig	180	192
Rat	2	0.3
Sheep	175	56
Sperm whale	7,800	13,500

ENDANGERED SPECIES

The World Conservation Union (WCU) categorises endangered species according to their rate of decline, population size, area of geographic distribution and degree of population and distribution fragmentation.

EX (Extinct): Dodo, Steller's Sea Cow
EW (Extinct in the Wild): Lonesome George, Wyoming toad
CR (Critically Endangered): Angel shark, jellyfish tree
EN (Endangered): chimpanzee, snow leopard
VU (Vulnerable): polar bear, common hippopotamus
NT (Near Threatened): Gentoo penguin, tiger shark
LC (Least Concern): house sparrow, brown pelican

The WCU's Red List is the most comprehensive information published on endangered species. Around 16,000 species of plants, animals, birds, reptiles etc are included each year. Species that appear on the 2006 Red List as critically endangered include:

African wild ass, black rhino, pygmy hog, Amur leopard, Bulmer's fruit bat, mountain gorilla, Eastern black crested gibbon, giant sea bass, Ganges shark, Himalayan quail
Countries with the most species appearing on the 2006 Red List:

Ecuador	2,180
United States	1,178
Malaysia	917
Indonesia	857
China	804

THE KINGDOM OF LIVING THINGS

Facts and figures about some record-breaking animals and plants

MAMMALS

Fastest mammal: cheetah (eastern and southern Africa) – up to 115 km/h (70mph)

Tallest mammal: giraffe (western and southern Africa) – up to 5.5m in height

Largest mammal: blue whale (Pacific, Indian and Southern oceans) – up to 33m in length

Largest land mammal: African bush elephant (central Africa) – up to 4.2m in height, 3.5m in length and 10,000kg in weight

Loudest mammal: blue whale – up to 188db

BIRDS

Fastest bird: peregrine falcon (worldwide) – up to 320 km/h (200mph)

Fastest land bird: ostrich (north Africa) – up to 65km/h (40mph)

Biggest wingspan: wandering albatross (Southern ocean) – up to 3.7m

Biggest flying creature: pterosaur – up to 20m

Longest migration: Arctic tern (Arctic and sub-Arctic regions) – average 35,000km (21,750 miles)

FISH AND REPTILES

Biggest fish: whale shark (Pacific, Atlantic and Indian oceans) – up to 12.5m in length

Biggest amphibian: Chinese giant salamander (China) – up to 1.8m in length

Biggest crocodile: estuarine or saltwater crocodile (south-east Asia, northern Australia) – up to 6m in length

Biggest spider: Goliath bird-eating spider (South America) – leg span of 30cm

Longest snake: reticulated python (south-east Asia) – up to 10m in length

PLANTS

Biggest living tree: Hyperion (Redwood National Park, Northern California) – 115.5m tall

Biggest tree: Lindsey Creek tree (Pacific Coast, USA) – trunk volume of 2549.6 cubic m, mass of 329,3136 kg

Biggest tree girth: European chestnut (Mount Etna, Sicily) – circumference of 58m

Fastest growing plant: bamboo (east Asia, Australia, sub-Saharan Africa, South America) – up to 1m per day

Longest roots: wild fig tree (east Asia, the Himalayas) – roots up to 120m

Biggest seed: double coconut or coco de mer (Seychelles) – up to 20 kg

Biggest leaves: raffia palm (Madagascar, South America, tropical Africa) – up to 21m long and 3m wide

SPORT

THE COMMONWEALTH GAMES

The Games were originally called the British Empire Games. From 1954 to 1966 the Games were known as the British Empire and Commonwealth Games, and from 1970 to 1974 as the British Commonwealth Games. Since 1978 the Games have been called the Commonwealth Games.

BRITISH EMPIRE GAMES
1930	Hamilton, Canada
1934	London, England
1938	Sydney, Australia
1950	Auckland, New Zealand

BRITISH EMPIRE AND COMMONWEALTH GAMES
1954	Vancouver, Canada
1958	Cardiff, Wales
1962	Perth, Australia
1966	Kingston, Jamaica

BRITISH COMMONWEALTH GAMES
1970	Edinburgh, Scotland
1974	Christchurch, New Zealand

COMMONWEALTH GAMES
1978	Edmonton, Canada
1982	Brisbane, Australia
1986	Edinburgh, Scotland
1990	Auckland, New Zealand
1994	Victoria, Canada
1998	Kuala Lumpur, Malaysia
2002	Manchester, England
2006	Melbourne, Australia
2010	Delhi, India

THE OLYMPIC GAMES

MODERN OLYMPIC GAMES
1896	Athens, Greece
1900	Paris, France
1904	St Louis, USA
1908	London, England
1912	Stockholm, Sweden
1920	Antwerp, Belgium
1924	Paris, France
1928	Amsterdam, Netherlands
1932	Los Angeles, USA
1936	Berlin, Germany
1948	London, England
1952	Helsinki, Finland
1956	Melbourne, Australia (equestrian events held in Stockholm, Sweden)
1960	Rome, Italy
1964	Tokyo, Japan
1968	Mexico City, Mexico
1972	Munich, West Germany
1976	Montreal, Canada
1980	Moscow, USSR
1984	Los Angeles, USA
1988	Seoul, South Korea
1992	Barcelona, Spain
1996	Atlanta, USA
2000	Sydney, Australia
2004	Athens, Greece
2008	Beijing, China
2012	London, UK

The following Games were scheduled but did not take place owing to World Wars:

1916	Berlin, Germany
1940	Tokyo, Japan; then Helsinki, Finland
1944	London, England

WINTER OLYMPIC GAMES

1924	Chamonix, France	1972	Sapporo, Japan
1928	St Moritz, Switzerland	1976	Innsbruck, Austria
1932	Lake Placid, USA	1980	Lake Placid, USA
1936	Garmisch-Partenkirchen, Germany	1984	Sarajevo, Yugoslavia
		1988	Calgary, Canada
1948	St Moritz, Switzerland	1992	Albertville, France
1952	Oslo, Norway	1994	Lillehammer, Norway
1956	Cortina d'Ampezzo, Italy	1998	Nagano, Japan
1960	Squaw Valley, USA	2002	Salt Lake City, USA
1964	Innsbruck, Austria	2006	Turin, Italy
1968	Grenoble, France	2010	Vancouver, Canada

ATHLETICS

WORLD RECORDS

MEN

Track

100m Asafa Powell (Jamaica) 2005/6	9.77sec
200m Michael Johnson (USA) 1996	19.32sec
400m Michael Johnson (USA) 1999	43.18sec
800m Wilson Kipketer (Denmark) 1997	1min 41.11sec
1,500m Hicham El Guerrouj (Morocco) 1998	3min 26.00sec
Marathon Paul Tergat (Kenya) 2003	2hr 04min 55sec
110m hurdles Liu Xiang (China) 2006	12.88sec
400m hurdles Kevin Young (USA) 1992	46.78sec

Field

High jump Javier Sotomayor (Cuba) 1993	2.45m
Pole vault Sergei Bubka (Ukraine) 1994	6.14m
Long jump Mike Powell (USA) 1991	8.95m
Triple jump Jonathan Edwards (GB) 1995	18.29m
Shot Randy Barnes (USA) 1980	23.12m
Discus Jurgen Schult (GDR) 1986	74.08m
Hammer Yuriy Sedykh (USSR) 1986	86.74m
Javelin Jan Zelezny (Czech Rep.) 1996	98.48m
Decathlon Roman Sebrle (Czech Rep.) 2001	9,026pts

WOMEN
Track

100m Florence Griffith-Joyner (USA) 1988		10.49sec
200m Florence Griffith-Joyner (USA) 1988		21.34sec
400m Marita Koch (GDR) 1985		47.60sec
800m Jarmila Kratochvilova (Czechoslovakia) 1983		1min 53.28sec
1,500m Qu Yunxia (China) 1993		3min 50.46sec
Marathon Paula Radcliffe (GB) 2003		2hr 15min 25sec
100m hurdles Yordanka Donkova (Bulgaria) 1988		12.21sec
400m hurdles Yulia Pechonkina (Russia) 2003		52.34sec

Field

High jump Stefka Kostadinova (Bulgaria) 1987		2.09m
Pole vault Yelena Isinbayeva (Russia) 2005		5.01m
Long jump Galina Chistiakova (USSR) 1988		7.52m
Triple jump Inessa Kravets (Ukraine) 1995		15.50m
Shot Natalya Lisovskaya (USSR) 1987		22.63m
Discus Gabriele Reinsch (GDR) 1988		76.80m
Hammer Tatyana Lysenko (Russia) 2006		77.80m
Javelin Osleidys Menendez (Cuba) 2005		71.70m
Heptathlon Jackie-Joyner Kersee (USA) 1986		7,291pts

LONDON MARATHON
First held 1981

YEAR	MEN	WOMEN
1981	Dick Beardsley (USA)	Joyce Smith (GB)
	Inge Simonson (Norway)	
1982	Hugh Jones (GB)	Joyce Smith (GB)
1983	Mike Gratton (GB)	Grete Waitz (Norway)
1984	Charlie Spedding (GB)	Ingrid Kristiansen (Norway)
1985	Steve Jones (GB)	Ingrid Kristiansen (Norway)
1986	Toshihiko Seko (Japan)	Grete Waitz (Norway)
1987	Hiromi Taniguchi (Japan)	Ingrid Kristiansen (Norway)
1988	Henrik Jorgensen (Denmark)	Ingrid Kristiansen (Norway)
1989	Douglas Wakiihuri (Kenya)	Veronique Marot (GB)
1990	Allister Hutton (GB)	Wanda Panfil (Poland)
1991	Yakov Tolstikov (EUN)	Rosa Mota (Portugal)
1992	Antonio Pinto (Portugal)	Katrin Dorre (Germany)
1993	Eamonn Martin (GB)	Katrin Dorre (Germany)
1994	Dionicio Ceron (Mexico)	Katrin Dorre (Germany)

YEAR	MEN	WOMEN
1995	Dionicio Ceron (Mexico)	Malgorzata Sobanska (Poland)
1996	Dionicio Ceron (Mexico)	Liz McColgan (GB)
1997	Antonio Pinto (Portugal)	Joyce Chepchumba (Kenya)
1998	Abel Anton (Spain)	Catherina McKiernan (Ireland)
1999	Abdelkader El Mouaziz (Morocco)	Joyce Chepchumba (Kenya)
2000	Antonio Pinto (Portugal)	Tegla Loroupe (Kenya)
2001	Abdelkader El Mouaziz (Morocco)	Deratu Tulu (Ethiopia)
2002	Khalid Khannouchi (USA)	Paula Radcliffe (GB)
2003	Gezahegne Abera (Ethiopia)	Paula Radcliffe (GB)
2004	Evans Rutto (Kenya)	Margaret Okayo (Kenya)
2005	Martin Lel (Kenya)	Paula Radcliffe (GB)
2006	Felix Limo (Kenya)	Deena Kastor (USA)
2007	Martin Lel (Kenya)	Zhou Chunxiu (China)

CRICKET

WORLD CUP WINNERS
First held 1975

YEAR	WINNER
1975	West Indies
1979	West Indies
1983	India
1987	Australia
1992	Pakistan
1996	Sri Lanka
1999	Australia
2003	Australia
2007	Australia

COUNTY CHAMPIONS
First held 1864

YEAR	WINNER
1980	Middlesex
1981	Nottinghamshire
1982	Middlesex
1983	Essex
1984	Essex
1985	Middlesex
1986	Essex
1987	Nottinghamshire
1988	Worcestershire
1989	Worcestershire
1990	Middlesex
1991	Essex
1992	Essex
1993	Middlesex
1994	Warwickshire
1995	Warwickshire
1996	Leicestershire
1997	Glamorgan
1998	Leicestershire
1999	Surrey
2000	Surrey
2001	Yorkshire
2002	Surrey
2003	Sussex
2004	Warwickshire
2005	Nottinghamshire
2006	Sussex

TEST CRICKET

Leading Batsmen

Brian Lara (West Indies)	11953 runs at an average of 52.88
Allan Border (Australia)	11174 at 50.56
Steve Waugh (Australia)	10927 at 51.06
Sachin Tendulkar (India)	10668 at 54.7
Sunil Gavaskar (India)	10122 at 51.12

Leading Bowlers

Shane Warne (Australia)	708 wickets at an average of 25.41
Muttiah Muralitharan (Sri Lanka)	674 at 21.73
Glenn McGrath (Australia)	563 at 21.64
Anil Kumble (India)	547 at 28.65
Courtney Walsh (West Indies)	519 at 24.44

Most Expensive Overs

Brian Lara (West Indies), b. Robin Peterson (South Africa), 2003–4	28 runs
Shahid Afridi (Pakistan), b. Harbhajan Singh (India), 2005–6	27 runs
Craig McMillan (New Zealand), b. Younis Khan (Pakistan), 2000–1	26 runs
Brian Lara (West Indies), b. Danish Kaneria (Pakistan), 2006–7	26 runs
Andy Roberts (West Indies), b. Ian Botham (England), 1980–1	25 runs

b. = bowled

FOOTBALL

WORLD CUP WINNERS

First held 1930

YEAR	VENUE	WINNER
1930	Uruguay	Uruguay
1934	Italy	Italy
1938	France	Italy
1950	Brazil	Uruguay
1954	Switzerland	West Germany
1958	Sweden	Brazil
1962	Chile	Brazil
1966	England	England
1970	Mexico	Brazil
1974	West Germany	West Germany
1978	Argentina	Argentina
1982	Spain	Italy
1986	Mexico	Argentina
1990	Italy	West Germany
1994	USA	Brazil
1998	France	France
2002	Korea/Japan	Brazil
2006	Germany	Italy

LEAGUE CHAMPIONS
First held 1889

YEAR	WINNER
1980	Liverpool
1981	Aston Villa
1982	Liverpool
1983	Liverpool
1984	Liverpool
1985	Everton
1986	Liverpool
1987	Everton
1988	Liverpool
1989	Arsenal
1990	Liverpool
1991	Arsenal
1992	Leeds United
1993	Manchester United
1994	Manchester United
1995	Blackburn Rovers
1996	Manchester United
1997	Manchester United
1998	Arsenal
1999	Manchester United
2000	Manchester United
2001	Manchester United
2002	Arsenal
2003	Manchester United
2004	Arsenal
2005	Chelsea
2006	Chelsea
2007	Manchester United

FA CUP WINNERS
First held 1872

YEAR	WINNER
1980	West Ham United
1981	Tottenham Hotspur
1982	Tottenham Hotspur
1983	Manchester United
1984	Everton
1985	Manchester United
1986	Liverpool
1987	Coventry
1988	Wimbledon
1989	Liverpool
1990	Manchester United
1991	Tottenham Hotspur
1992	Liverpool
1993	Arsenal
1994	Manchester United
1995	Everton
1996	Manchester United
1997	Chelsea
1998	Arsenal
1999	Manchester United
2000	Chelsea
2001	Liverpool
2002	Arsenal
2003	Arsenal
2004	Manchester United
2005	Arsenal
2006	Liverpool
2007	Chelsea

FOOTBALL GROUNDS OF ENGLAND

STADIUM	TEAM
Anfield	Liverpool
Boleyn Ground (Upton Park)	West Ham United
Bramall Lane	Sheffield United
City Ground	Nottingham Forest
City of Manchester Stadium	Manchester City
Elland Road	Leeds United
Emirates Stadium	Arsenal
Ewood Park	Blackburn Rovers
Goodison Park	Everton
Hillsborough	Sheffield Wednesday
Old Trafford	Manchester United
Portman Road	Ipswich Town
Pride Park	Derby County
Riverside Stadium	Middlesbrough
St Andrews	Birmingham City
St James' Park	Newcastle United
St Mary's Stadium	Southampton
Stadium of Light	Sunderland
Stamford Bridge	Chelsea
Villa Park	Aston Villa
Walkers Stadium	Leicester City
Wembley Stadium	—
White Hart Lane	Tottenham Hotspur

GOLF

MAJORS*

Jack Nicklaus (USA)	18
Tiger Woods (USA)	12
Walter Hagen (USA)	11
Ben Hogan (USA)	9
Gary Player (South Africa)	9

* Majors = Masters, US Open, British Open, PGA

OPEN CHAMPIONS

First held 1860
Played over 72 holes since 1892

YEAR	WINNER
1980	Tom Watson (USA)
1981	Bill Rogers (USA)
1982	Tom Watson (USA)
1983	Tom Watson (USA)
1984	Severiano Ballesteros (Spain)
1985	Sandy Lyle (GB)
1986	Greg Norman (Australia)
1987	Nick Faldo (GB)
1988	Severiano Ballesteros (Spain)
1989	Mark Calcavecchia (USA)
1990	Nick Faldo (GB)
1991	Ian Baker-Finch (Australia)
1992	Nick Faldo (GB)
1993	Greg Norman (Australia)
1994	Nick Price (Zimbabwe)
1995	John Daly (USA)
1996	Tom Lehman (USA)
1997	Justin Leonard (USA)
1998	Mark O'Meara (USA)
1999	Paul Lawrie (GB)
2000	Tiger Woods (USA)
2001	David Duval (USA)
2002	Ernie Els (South Africa)
2003	Ben Curtis (USA)
2004	Todd Hamilton (USA)
2005	Tiger Woods (USA)
2006	Tiger Woods (USA)

RYDER CUP WINNERS

First held 1927. Played over 2 days
1927–61; over 3 days 1963 to date

YEAR	WINNER
1981	USA
1983	USA
1985	Great Britain and Europe
1987	Great Britain and Europe

1989	Match drawn
1991	USA
1993	USA
1995	Europe
1997	Europe
1999	USA
2002	Europe
2004	Europe
2006	Europe

US OPEN CHAMPIONS

First held 1895

YEAR	WINNER
1980	Jack Nicklaus (USA)
1981	David Graham (Australia)
1982	Tom Watson (USA)
1983	Larry Nelson (USA)
1984	Fuzzy Zoeller (USA)
1985	Andy North (USA)
1986	Raymond Floyd (USA)
1987	Scott Simpson (USA)
1988	Curtis Strange (USA)
1989	Curtis Strange (USA)
1990	Hale Irwin (USA)
1991	Payne Stewart (USA)
1992	Tom Kite (USA)
1993	Lee Janzen (USA)
1994	Ernie Els (South Africa)
1995	Corey Pavin (USA)
1996	Steve Jones (USA)
1997	Ernie Els (South Africa)
1998	Lee Janzen (USA)
1999	Payne Stewart (USA)
2000	Tiger Woods (USA)
2001	Retief Goosen (South Africa)
2002	Tiger Woods (USA)
2003	Jim Furyk (USA)
2004	Retief Goosen (South Africa)
2005	Michael Campbell (New Zealand)
2006	Geoff Ogilvy (Australia)
2007	Angel Cabrera (Argentina)

US MASTERS CHAMPIONS

First held 1934

YEAR	WINNER
1980	Severiano Ballesteros (Spain)
1981	Tom Watson (USA)
1982	Craig Stadler (USA)
1983	Severiano Ballesteros (Spain)
1984	Ben Crenshaw (USA)
1985	Bernhard Langer (W. Germany)
1986	Jack Nicklaus (USA)
1987	Larry Mize (USA)
1988	Sandy Lyle (GB)
1989	Nick Faldo (GB)
1990	Nick Faldo (GB)
1991	Ian Woosnam (GB)
1992	Fred Couples (USA)
1993	Bernhard Langer (Germany)
1994	José María Olazábal (Spain)
1995	Ben Crenshaw (USA)
1996	Nick Faldo (GB)
1997	Tiger Woods (USA)
1998	Mark O'Meara (USA)
1999	José María Olazábal (Spain)
2000	Vijay Singh (Fiji)
2001	Tiger Woods (USA)
2002	Tiger Woods (USA)
2003	Mike Weir (Canada)
2004	Phil Mickelson (USA)
2005	Tiger Woods (USA)
2006	Phil Mickelson (USA)
2007	Zach Johnson (USA)

HORSE RACING

DERBY WINNERS

First run in 1780

YEAR	WINNING HORSE
1980	Henbit
1981	Shergar

1982   Golden Fleece
1983   Teenoso
1984   Secreto
1985   Slip Anchor
1986   Shahrastani
1987   Reference Point
1988   Kahyasi
1989   Nashwan
1990   Quest for Fame
1991   Generous
1992   Dr Devious
1993   Commander In Chief
1994   Erhaab
1995   Lammtarra
1996   Shaamit
1997   Benny The Dip
1998   High Rise
1999   Oath
2000   Sinndar
2001   Galileo
2002   High Chaparral
2003   Kris Kin
2004   North Light
2005   Motivator
2006   Sir Percy
2007   Authorized

GRAND NATIONAL WINNERS

First run in 1839

YEAR	WINNING HORSE
1980	Ben Nevis
1981	Aldaniti
1982	Grittar
1983	Corbiere
1984	Hallo Dandy
1985	Last Suspect
1986	West Tip
1987	Maori Venture
1988	Rhyme 'N' Reason

1989   Little Polveir
1990   Mr Frisk
1991   Seagram
1992   Party Politics
1993   *Race declared void*
1994   Miinnehoma
1995   Royal Athlete
1996   Rough Quest
1997   Lord Gyllene
1998   Earth Summit
1999   Bobbyjo
2000   Papillon
2001   Red Marauder
2002   Bindaree
2003   Monty's Pass
2004   Amberleigh House
2005   Hedgehunter
2006   Numbersixvalverde
2007   Silver Birch

MOTOR RACING

FORMULA ONE WORLD CHAMPIONS

First held 1950

YEAR	WINNER
1980	Alan Jones (Australia)
1981	Nelson Piquet (Brazil)
1982	Keke Rosberg (Finland)
1983	Nelson Piquet (Brazil)
1984	Niki Lauda (Austria)
1985	Alain Prost (France)
1986	Alain Prost (France)
1987	Nelson Piquet (Brazil)
1988	Ayrton Senna (Brazil)
1989	Alain Prost (France)
1990	Ayrton Senna (Brazil)
1991	Ayrton Senna (Brazil)
1992	Nigel Mansell (GB)
1993	Alain Prost (France)

1994	Michael Schumacher (Germany)
1995	Michael Schumacher (Germany)
1996	Damon Hill (GB)
1997	Jacques Villeneuve (Canada)
1998	Mika Hakkinen (Finland)
1999	Mika Hakkinen (Finland)
2000	Michael Schumacher (Germany)
2001	Michael Schumacher (Germany)
2002	Michael Schumacher (Germany)
2003	Michael Schumacher (Germany)
2004	Michael Schumacher (Germany)
2005	Fernando Alonso (Spain)
2006	Fernando Alonso (Spain)

ROWING

THE UNIVERSITY BOAT RACE

First held 1829
1829–2007: Cambridge 79 wins, Oxford 73; one dead heat (1877)

YEAR	WINNER
1980	Oxford
1981	Oxford
1982	Oxford
1983	Oxford
1984	Oxford
1985	Oxford
1986	Cambridge
1987	Oxford
1988	Oxford
1989	Oxford
1990	Oxford
1991	Oxford
1992	Oxford
1993	Cambridge
1994	Cambridge
1995	Cambridge
1996	Cambridge
1997	Cambridge
1998	Cambridge
1999	Cambridge
2000	Oxford
2001	Oxford
2002	Oxford
2003	Oxford
2004	Cambridge
2005	Oxford
2006	Oxford
2007	Cambridge

RUGBY LEAGUE

WORLD CUP WINNERS

First held 1954

YEAR	WINNER
1954	Great Britain
1957	Australia
1960	Great Britain
1968	Australia
1970	Australia
1972	Great Britain
1975	Australia
1977	Australia
1988	Australia
1992	Australia
1995	Australia
2000	Australia

CHALLENGE CUP WINNERS

First held 1897

YEAR	WINNER
1980	Hull Kingston Rovers
1981	Widnes
1982	Hull
1983	Featherstone Rovers
1984	Widnes

1985	Wigan
1986	Castleford
1987	Halifax
1988	Wigan
1989	Wigan
1990	Wigan
1991	Wigan
1992	Wigan
1993	Wigan
1994	Wigan
1995	Wigan
1996	St Helens
1997	St Helens
1998	Sheffield
1999	Leeds
2000	Bradford
2001	St Helens
2002	Wigan Warriors
2003	Bradford Bulls
2004	St Helens
2005	Hull
2006	St Helens

RUGBY UNION

WORLD CUP WINNERS

First held 1987

YEAR	WINNER
1987	New Zealand
1991	Australia
1995	South Africa
1999	Australia
2003	England

FOUR/FIVE/SIX NATIONS CHAMPIONS

First held 1883

YEAR	WINNER
1980	England
1981	France

1982	Ireland
1983	France/Ireland
1984	Scotland
1985	Ireland
1986	France/Scotland
1987	France
1988	Wales/France
1989	France
1990	Scotland
1991	England
1992	England
1993	France
1994	Wales
1995	England
1996	England
1997	France
1998	France
1999	Scotland
2000	England
2001	England
2002	France
2003	England
2004	France
2005	Wales
2006	France
2007	France

SNOOKER

WORLD PROFESSIONAL CHAMPIONS

First held 1927

YEAR	WINNER
1980	Cliff Thorburn (Canada)
1981	Steve Davis (England)
1982	Alex Higgins (N. Ireland)
1983	Steve Davis (England)
1984	Steve Davis (England)
1985	Dennis Taylor (N. Ireland)
1986	Joe Johnson (England)

1987	Steve Davis (England)
1988	Steve Davis (England)
1989	Steve Davis (England)
1990	Stephen Hendry (Scotland)
1991	John Parrott (England)
1992	Stephen Hendry (Scotland)
1993	Stephen Hendry (Scotland)
1994	Stephen Hendry (Scotland)
1995	Stephen Hendry (Scotland)
1996	Stephen Hendry (Scotland)
1997	Ken Doherty (Ireland)
1998	John Higgins (Scotland)
1999	Stephen Hendry (Scotland)
2000	Mark Williams (Wales)
2001	Ronnie O'Sullivan (England)
2002	Peter Ebdon (England)
2003	Mark Williams (Wales)
2004	Ronnie O'Sullivan (England)
2005	Shaun Murphy (England)
2006	Graeme Dott (Scotland)
2007	John Higgins (Scotland)

FASTEST 147 BREAKS

1.	Ronnie O'Sullivan (vs Mick Price)	21 April 1997	5min 20sec
2.	Ronnie O'Sullivan (vs Marco Fu)	22 April 2003	6min 30sec
3.	Ronnie O'Sullivan (vs Drew Henry)	17 October 2001	6min 36sec

TENNIS

WORLD RANKINGS

Highest number of weeks spent as world number one

MEN (since 1973)

	WEEKS
Pete Sampras (USA)	286
Ivan Lendl (Czech Republic)	270
Jimmy Connors (USA)	268
Roger Federer (Switzerland)†	170
John McEnroe (USA)	170

WOMEN (since 1975)

	WEEKS
Steffi Graf (Germany)	377
Martina Navratilova (USA)	331
Chris Evert (USA)	262
Martina Hingis (Switzerland)	209
Monica Seles (USA)	178

† = current world number one

WIMBLEDON MEN'S SINGLES CHAMPIONS

First held 1877

YEAR	WINNER
1980	Bjorn Borg (Sweden)
1981	John McEnroe (USA)
1982	Jimmy Connors (USA)
1983	John McEnroe (USA)
1984	John McEnroe (USA)
1985	Boris Becker (W. Germany)
1986	Boris Becker (W. Germany)
1987	Pat Cash (Australia)
1988	Stefan Edberg (Sweden)
1989	Boris Becker (W. Germany)
1990	Stefan Edberg (Sweden)
1991	Michael Stich (Germany)
1992	Andre Agassi (USA)
1993	Pete Sampras (USA)
1994	Pete Sampras (USA)
1995	Pete Sampras (USA)

1996	Richard Krajicek (Netherlands)
1997	Pete Sampras (USA)
1998	Pete Sampras (USA)
1999	Pete Sampras (USA)
2000	Pete Sampras (USA)
2001	Goran Ivanisevic (Croatia)
2002	Lleyton Hewitt (Australia)
2003	Roger Federer (Switzerland)
2004	Roger Federer (Switzerland)
2005	Roger Federer (Switzerland)
2006	Roger Federer (Switzerland)
2007	Roger Federer (Switzerland)

WIMBLEDON WOMEN'S SINGLES CHAMPIONS

First held 1884

YEAR	WINNER
1980	Evonne Cawley (Australia)
1981	Chris Evert Lloyd (USA)
1982	Martina Navratilova (USA)
1983	Martina Navratilova (USA)
1984	Martina Navratilova (USA)
1985	Martina Navratilova (USA)
1986	Martina Navratilova (USA)
1987	Martina Navratilova (USA)
1988	Steffi Graf (W. Germany)
1989	Steffi Graf (W. Germany)
1990	Martina Navratilova (USA)
1991	Steffi Graf (Germany)
1992	Steffi Graf (Germany)
1993	Steffi Graf (Germany)
1994	Conchita Martinez (Spain)
1995	Steffi Graf (Germany)
1996	Steffi Graf (Germany)
1997	Martina Hingis (Switzerland)
1998	Jana Novotna (Czech Republic)
1999	Lindsay Davenport (USA)
2000	Venus Williams (USA)
2001	Venus Williams (USA)
2002	Serena Williams (USA)
2003	Serena Williams (USA)
2004	Maria Sharapova (Russia)
2005	Venus Williams (USA)
2006	Amelie Mauresmo (France)
2007	Venus Williams (USA)

TIME

TIME ZONES

Standard time differences from the
Greenwich meridian

+ hours ahead of GMT
− hours behind GMT
* may vary from standard time at some
    part of the year (Summer Time or
    Daylight Saving Time)
† some areas may keep another time
    zone
h hours
m minutes

	h	m
Afghanistan	+ 4	30
*Albania	+ 1	
Algeria	+ 1	
*Andorra	+ 1	
Angola	+ 1	
Antigua and Barbuda	− 4	
Argentina	− 3	
*Armenia	+ 4	
*Australia		
*ACT, NSW (except Broken		
Hill area), Tas, Vic,		
Whitsunday Islands	+ 10	
Northern Territory	+ 9	30
Queensland	+ 10	
*South Australia	+ 9	30
*Western Australia	+ 8	
Christmas Island (Indian		
Ocean)	+ 7	
Cocos (Keeling) Islands	+ 6	30
Norfolk Island	+ 11	30
*Austria	+ 1	
*Azerbaijan	+ 4	
*Bahamas	− 5	
Bahrain	+ 3	

	h	m
Bangladesh	+ 6	
Barbados	− 4	
*Belarus	+ 2	
*Belgium	+ 1	
Belize	− 6	
Benin	+ 1	
Bhutan	+ 6	
Bolivia	− 4	
*Bosnia and Hercegovina	+ 1	
Botswana	+ 2	
*Brazil		
western states	− 5	
central states	− 4	
N. and N. E. coastal states	− 2	
*S. and E. coastal states,		
including Brasilia	− 3	
Fernando de Noronha		
Island	− 2	
Brunei	+ 8	
*Bulgaria	+ 2	
Burkina Faso	0	
Burundi	+ 2	
Cambodia	+ 7	
Cameroon	+ 1	
*Canada		
*Alberta	− 7	
*†British Columbia	− 8	
*Manitoba	− 6	
*New Brunswick	− 4	
*†Newfoundland	− 3	30
*†Northwest Territories	− 7	
*Nova Scotia	− 4	
*Nunavut		
central	− 6	
eastern	− 5	
mountain	− 7	
*Ontario		
east of 90° W.	− 5	
west of 90° W.	− 6	
*Prince Edward Island	− 4	

	h	m
*Québec		
east of 63° W.	− 4	
*west of 63° W.	− 5	
*†Saskatchewan	− 6	
*Yukon	− 8	
Cape Verde	− 1	
Central African Republic	+ 1	
Chad	+ 1	
*Chile	− 4	
China (inc. Hong Kong and		
Macao)	+ 8	
Colombia	− 5	
The Comoros	+ 3	
Congo, Dem. Rep. of		
Haut-Zaïre, Kasai,		
Kivu, Shaba	+ 2	
Kinshasa, Mbandaka	+ 1	
Congo, Republic of	+ 1	
Costa Rica	− 6	
Côte d'Ivoire	0	
*Croatia	+ 1	
*Cuba	− 5	
*Cyprus	+ 2	
*Czech Republic	+ 1	
*Denmark	+ 1	
*Faeroe Islands	0	
*Greenland	− 3	
Danmarks Havn,		
Mesters Vig	0	
*Scoresby Sund	− 1	
*Thule area	− 4	
Djibouti	+ 3	
Dominica	− 4	
Dominican Republic	− 4	
East Timor	+ 9	
Ecuador	− 5	
Galápagos Islands	− 6	
*Egypt	+ 2	
El Salvador	− 6	
Equatorial Guinea	+ 1	
Eritrea	+ 3	

	h	m
*Estonia	+ 2	
Ethiopia	+ 3	
Fiji	+ 12	
*Finland	+ 2	
*France	+ 1	
French Guiana	− 3	
French Polynesia	− 10	
Guadeloupe	− 4	
Marquesas Islands	− 9	30
Martinique	− 4	
New Caledonia	+ 11	
Réunion	+ 4	
*St Pierre and Miquelon	− 3	
Wallis and Futuna	+ 12	
Gabon	+ 1	
The Gambia	0	
Georgia	+ 4	
*Germany	+ 1	
Ghana	0	
*Greece	+ 2	
Grenada	− 4	
*Guatemala	− 6	
Guinea	0	
Guinea-Bissau	0	
Guyana	− 4	
*Haiti	− 5	
Honduras	− 6	
*Hungary	+ 1	
Iceland	0	
India	+ 5	30
Indonesia		
Java, Kalimantan (west and		
central), Madura, Sumatra	+ 7	
Bali, Flores, Kalimantan		
(south and east), Lombok,		
Sulawesi, Sumbawa,		
West Timor	+ 8	
Irian Jaya, Maluku	+ 9	
Iran	+ 3	30
*Iraq	+ 3	
*Ireland, Republic of	0	

	h	m		h	m
*Israel	+ 2		Chuuk, Yap	+ 10	
*Italy	+ 1		Kosrae, Pingelap,		
Jamaica	− 5		Pohnpei	+ 11	
Japan	+ 9		*Moldova	+ 2	
*Jordan	+ 2		*Monaco	+ 1	
Kazakhstan			*†Mongolia	+ 8	
western	+ 5		*Montenegro	+ 1	
eastern	+ 6		Morocco	0	
Kenya	+ 3		Mozambique	+ 2	
Kiribati	+ 12		Myanmar	+ 6	30
Line Islands	+ 14		*Namibia	+ 1	
Phoenix Islands	+ 13		Nauru	+ 12	
Korea, Dem. People's Rep. of	+ 9		Nepal	+ 5	45
Korea, Republic of	+ 9		*The Netherlands	+ 1	
Kuwait	+ 3		Aruba	− 4	
Kyrgyzstan	+ 6		Netherlands Antilles	− 4	
Laos	+ 7		*New Zealand	+ 12	
*Latvia	+ 2		Cook Islands	− 10	
*Lebanon	+ 2		Niue	− 11	
Lesotho	+ 2		Tokelau Island	− 10	
Liberia	0		Nicaragua	− 6	
Libya	+ 2		Niger	+ 1	
*Liechtenstein	+ 1		Nigeria	+ 1	
*Lithuania	+ 2		*Norway	+ 1	
*Luxembourg	+ 1		*Svalbard, Jan Mayen	+ 1	
*Macedonia	+ 1		Oman	+ 4	
Madagascar	+ 3		Pakistan	+ 5	
Malawi	+ 2		Palau	+ 9	
Malaysia	+ 8		Panama	− 5	
Maldives	+ 5		Papua New Guinea	+ 10	
Mali	0		*Paraguay	− 4	
*Malta	+ 1		Peru	− 5	
Marshall Islands	+ 12		The Philippines	+ 8	
Mauritania	0		*Poland	+ 1	
Mauritius	+ 4		*Portugal	0	
*Mexico	− 6		*Azores	− 1	
*Nayarit, Sinaloa, S. Baja			*Madeira	0	
California	− 7		Qatar	+ 3	
*N. Baja California	− 8		*Romania	+ 2	
Sonora	− 7		*Russia		
Micronesia, Fed. States of			Zone 1	+ 2	

	h	m
Zone 2	+ 3	
Zone 3	+ 4	
Zone 4	+ 5	
Zone 5	+ 6	
Zone 6	+ 7	
Zone 7	+ 8	
Zone 8	+ 9	
Zone 9	+ 10	
Zone 10	+ 11	
Zone 11	+ 12	
Rwanda	+ 2	
St Christopher and Nevis	− 4	
St Lucia	− 4	
St Vincent and the Grenadines	− 4	
Samoa	− 11	
*San Marino	+ 1	
São Tomé and Príncipe	0	
Saudi Arabia	+ 3	
Senegal	0	
*Serbia	+ 1	
Seychelles	+ 4	
Sierra Leone	0	
Singapore	+ 8	
*Slovakia	+ 1	
*Slovenia	+ 1	
Solomon Islands	+ 11	
Somalia	+ 3	
South Africa	+ 2	
*Spain	+ 1	
*Canary Islands	0	
Sri Lanka	+ 5	30
Sudan	+ 3	
Suriname	− 3	
Swaziland	+ 2	
*Sweden	+ 1	
*Switzerland	+ 1	
*Syria	+ 2	
Taiwan	+ 8	
Tajikistan	+ 5	
Tanzania	+ 3	
Thailand	+ 7	

	h	m
Togo	0	
Tonga	+ 13	
Trinidad and Tobago	− 4	
*Tunisia	+ 1	
*Turkey	+ 2	
Turkmenistan	+ 5	
Tuvalu	+ 12	
Uganda	+ 3	
*Ukraine	+ 2	
United Arab Emirates	+ 4	
*United Kingdom	0	
Anguilla	− 4	
*Bermuda	− 4	
†British Antarctic Territory	− 3	
British Indian Ocean Territory	+ 5	
British Virgin Islands	− 4	
Cayman Islands	− 5	
*Falkland Islands	− 4	
*Gibraltar	+ 1	
Montserrat	− 4	
Pitcairn Islands	− 8	
St Helena and Dependencies	0	
South Georgia Islands	− 2	
*Turks and Caicos Islands	− 5	
*United States of America		
*Alaska	− 9	
Aleutian Islands, east of 169° 30′ W.	− 9	
Aleutian Islands, west of 169° 30′ W.	− 10	
*central time	− 6	
*eastern time	− 5	
Guam	+ 10	
Hawaii	− 10	
*mountain time	− 7	
Northern Mariana Islands	+ 10	
*Pacific time	− 8	
Puerto Rico	− 4	
Samoa, American	− 11	

	h	m		h	m
Virgin Islands	− 4		Venezuela	− 4	
*Uruguay	− 3		Vietnam	+ 7	
Uzbekistan	+ 5		Yemen	+ 3	
Vanuatu	+ 11		Zambia	+ 2	
*Vatican City State	+ 1		Zimbabwe	+ 2	

TIME MEASUREMENT

Measurements of time are based on the time taken:

by the Earth to rotate on its axis (day)

by the Moon to revolve around the Earth (month)

by the Earth to revolve around the Sun from equinox to equinox (year)

The orbits on which these timescales are based are not uniform, so average or mean periods have been adopted for everyday use.

PERIOD	ACTUAL LENGTH	MEAN LENGTH
Day	23 hours, 56 minutes, 4 seconds	24 hours, each of 60 minutes
Month (from New Moon to New Moon)	29 days, 12 hours, 44 minutes	varies from 28 to 31 days
Year (tropical)	365 days, 5 hours, 48 minutes, 45 seconds	365 days (366 in leap years), each of 24 hours

LEAP YEARS

The tropical year (the period of the Earth's orbit around the Sun) is 365 days 6 hours minus about 11 minutes 15 seconds. Because of the difference between the length of the tropical year and the mean year used for calendar purposes, the natural timescale and the calendar get out of step by 11 minutes 15 seconds each year. The growing difference between the two is corrected by having a leap year every four years.

However, a leap year brings the calendar back by 45 minutes too much. To correct this, the last year of a century is in most cases not a leap year, but the omission corrects the calendar by six hours too much; compensation for this is made by every fourth end-century year being a leap year.

A year is a leap year if the date of the year is divisible by four without remainder, unless it is the last year of the century. The last year of the century is a leap year if the date of the year is divisible by 400 without remainder, eg the years 1800 and 1900 were not leap years but the year 2000 was a leap year.

THE SEASONS

Because the Earth's axis is tilted at 66.5° to the plane in which it orbits the Sun, each hemisphere alternately leans towards or away from the Sun, causing the seasons. The seasons are defined as:

SEASON	ASTRONOMICAL DEFINITION	POPULAR DEFINITION
Spring	vernal equinox to summer solstice	March, April, May
Summer	summer solstice to autumnal equinox	June, July, August
Autumn	autumnal equinox to winter solstice	September, October, November
Winter	winter solstice to vernal equinox	December, January, February

THE SOLSTICE

A solstice is the point in the tropical year at which the Sun is at its greatest distance north or south of the Equator. In the northern hemisphere, the furthest point north is the summer solstice (longest day) and the furthest point south is the winter solstice (shortest day).

THE EQUINOX

The equinox is the point at which the Sun crosses the Equator and day and night are of equal length all over the world. This occurs around 20 or 21 March (vernal equinox) and 22 or 23 September (autumnal equinox).

CALENDARS

The year-numbering system and the calendar now used more or less world-wide are those of western Europe, ie Christian chronology and the Gregorian calendar.

CHRISTIAN CHRONOLOGY

The Christian era is numbered from the birth of Christ. Years after the birth of Christ are denoted by AD (*Anno Domini* – In the Year of Our Lord). Years before the birth of Christ are denoted by the letters BC (Before Christ) or, more rarely, AC (*Ante Christum*). The actual date of the birth of Christ is uncertain.

The system was introduced into Italy in the sixth century. Though first used in France in the seventh century, it did not become universally used there until the eighth century. The system was reputedly introduced into England by St Augustine in the sixth century, but it was not generally used until the Council of Chelsea (AD 816) ordered its use.

THE GREGORIAN CALENDAR

The Gregorian calendar is based on the Julian calendar adopted in the Roman Republic in 45 BC at the instigation of Julius Caesar (*see* Roman Calendar). The Julian calendar had a year of 365 days, with a leap year of 366 days every four years, including the last year of each century.

Because the end-century years in the Julian calendar were leap years, by the end of the 16th century there was a difference of ten days between the tropical year and the calendar year; the vernal equinox fell on 11 March. In 1582 Pope Gregory ordained that 5 October should be called 15 October and that of the end-century years only the fourth should be a leap year.

NAMES OF THE DAYS
The names of the days are derived from Old English translations or adaptations of the Roman names of the Sun, Moon and five planets:

DAY	OLD ENGLISH DERIVATION	ROMAN NAME
Sunday	Sun	Sol
Monday	Moon	Luna
Tuesday	Tiw/Tyr (god of war)	Mars
Wednesday	Woden/Odin	Mercury
Thursday	Thor	Jupiter
Friday	Frigga/Freyja (goddess of love)	Venus
Saturday	Saeternes	Saturn

NAMES OF THE MONTHS
The names of the months are derived from the pre-Julian Roman calendar, which originally had a year of ten months, beginning with March. Two months, January and February, were subsequently added to make a year of 12 months.

MONTH	DERIVATION
January	*Janus*, god of the portal, facing two ways, past and future
February	*Februa*, the Roman festival of purification
March	*Mars*, god of battle
April	*Aperire*, to open; the Earth opens to receive seed
May	*Maia*, goddess of growth and increase
June	*Junius*, the Romangens (family)
July	the emperor *Julius* Caesar (originally Quintilis, the fifth month)
August	the emperor *Augustus* (originally Sextilis, the sixth month)
September	*Septem*, the seventh month (of the original Roman calendar)
October	*Octo*, the eighth month
November	*Novem*, the ninth month
December	*Decem*, the tenth month

RELIGIOUS CALENDARS
CHRISTIAN

The Roman Catholic and Protestant Churches use the Gregorian calendar. The Church year begins with the first Sunday in the season of Advent and its principal seasons are:

Advent	preparation for Christmas
Christmas	celebration of the birth of Jesus Christ
Epiphany	celebration of the manifestation of Jesus Christ
Lent	preparation for Easter
Easter	celebration of the death and resurrection of Jesus Christ

The principal feasts and holy days in the Church of England are:

Christmas Day	25 December
The Epiphany	6 January
Presentation of Christ in the Temple	2 February
Ash Wednesday	first day of Lent, 40 days before Easter Day
Annunciation to the Blessed Virgin Mary	25 March
Maundy Thursday	Thursday before Easter Day
Good Friday	Friday before Easter Day
Easter Day*	date varies according to the Moon
Ascension Day	40 days after Easter Day
Pentecost (Whit Sunday)	nine days after Ascension Day
Trinity Sunday	Sunday after Pentecost
All Saints' Day	1 November

*Easter Day can fall at the earliest on 22 March and at the latest on 25 April.

THE EASTERN ORTHODOX CHURCHES
Some of the Eastern Orthodox Churches
use the Julian calendar and some a
modified version of the Julian calendar.
The Orthodox Church year begins on 1
September. There are four fast periods
and, in addition to Pascha (Easter) 12
great feasts, as well as commemorations
of the saints of the Old and New
Testaments throughout the year.

HINDU
The Hindu calendar is a luni-solar
calendar of 12 months, each containing
29 days 12 hours. Each month is divided
into a light fortnight (Shukla or
Shuddha) and a dark fortnight (Krishna
or Vadya) based on the waxing and
waning of the Moon. A leap month

occurs about every 32 lunar months,
whenever the difference between the
Hindu year of 360 lunar days (354 days
8 hours solar time) and the 365 days 6
hours of the solar year reaches the length
of one Hindu lunar month (29 days 12
hours).

The names of the days of the week are
derived from the Sanskrit names of the
Sun, the Moon and the planets Mars,
Mercury, Jupiter, Venus and Saturn. The
months have Sanskrit names derived
from 12 asterisms (constellations).

The days are: Raviwar, Somawar,
Mangalwar, Budhawar, Guruwar,
Shukrawar and Shaniwar. The months
are: Chaitra, Vaishakh, Jyeshtha, Ashadh,
Shravan, Bhadrapad, Ashvin, Kartik,
Margashirsh, Paush, Magh and Phalgun.

The major festivals are:

Chaitra	Spring New Year
Dasara*	victory of Rama over the demon army
Diwali*	New Year (festival of lights)
Durga-puja*	dedicated to the goddess Durga
Ganesh Chaturthi*	worship of Ganesh
Holi*	spring festival
Janmashtami*	birth festival of the god Krishna
Makara Sankranti	winter solstice festival
Navaratri*	nine-night festival dedicated to the goddess Parvati
Raksha-bandhan*	renewal of kinship bond between brothers and sisters
Ramanavami*	birth festival of the god Rama
Sarasvati-puja*	dedicated to the goddess Sarasvati
Shivatatri	dedicated to the god Shiva

* The main festivals celebrated by Hindus in the UK

JEWISH

The epoch, or starting point, of Jewish chronology corresponds to 7 October 3761 BC. The calendar is luni-solar; the hour is divided into 1,080 minims and the period between one New Moon and the next is reckoned as 29 days 12 hours 793 minims.

The Jewish day begins between sunset and nightfall. The time used is that of the meridian of Jerusalem, which is 2 hours 21 minutes in advance of GMT. Rules for the beginning of sabbaths and festivals were laid down for the latitude of London in the 18th century; hours for nightfall are now fixed annually by the Chief Rabbi.

A Jewish year is one of six types:

Minimal Common	353 days
Regular Common	354 days
Full Common	355 days
Minimal Leap	383 days
Regular Leap	384 days
Full Leap	385 days

Regular year	alternate months of 30 and 29 days
Full year	the second month has 30 instead of 29 days
Minimal year	the third month has 29 instead of 30 days
Leap year	an additional month of 30 days (Adar I) precedes the month of Adar, which in leap years also has 30 days

The months are: Tishri (30 days), Marcheshvan (29/30), Kislev (30/29), Tebet (29), Shebat (30), Adar (29), Nisan (30), Iyar (29), Sivan (30), Tammuz (29), Ab (30) and Elul (29).

The main festivals are:

Rosh Hashanah (New Year)
Fast of Gedaliah
Yom Kippur (Day of Atonement)
Succoth (Feast of Tabernacles)
Hoshana Rabba
Shemini Atseret (Solemn Assembly)
Simchat Torah (Rejoicing of the Law)
Chanucah (Dedication of the Temple)

Fast of Tebet
Fast of Esther
Purim (Festival of Lots)
Shusham Purim
Pesach (Passover)
Shavuot (Feast of Weeks)
Fast of Tammuz
Fast of Ab

MUSLIM

The Muslim era is dated from the Hijrah, or flight of the Prophet Muhammad from Mecca to Medina; the date corresponds to 16 July AD 622. The calendar is based on a lunar year of about 354 days, consisting of 12 months containing alternate months of 30 and 29 days. A leap day is added at the end of the 12th month at stated intervals in each cycle of 30 years. The purpose of the leap day is to reconcile the date of the first day of the month with the date of the actual New Moon. In each cycle of 30 years, 19 years are common (354 days) and 11 years are leap (kabisah) years (355 days).

Some Muslims still take the date of the evening of the first physical sighting of the crescent of the New Moon as that of the first of the month. If cloud obscures the Moon the present month may be extended to 30 days, after which the new month will begin automatically regardless of whether the Moon has been seen.

The months are: Muharram (30 days), Safar (29), Rabi' I (30), Rabi' II (29), Jumada I (30), Jumada II (29), Rajab (30), Sha'ban (29), Ramadan (30), Shawwâl (29), Dhû'l-Qa'da (30) and Dhû'l-Hijjah (29).

The main festivals are:

Eid-ul-Fitr	marks the end of Ramadan
Eid-ul-Adha	celebrates the submission of the Prophet Ibrahim (Abraham) to God
Ashura	the day Prophet Noah left the Ark and Prophet Moses was saved from Pharaoh (Sunni)
	death of the Prophet's grandson Husain (Shi'ite)
Mawlid al-Nabi	birthday of the Prophet Muhammad
Laylat al-Isra' wa'l-Mi'raj	Night of Journey and Ascension
Laylat al-Qadr	Night of Power

SIKH

The Sikh calendar is a lunar calendar of 365 days divided into 12 months. The length of the months varies between 29 and 32 days.

The main celebrations are:

Baisakhi Mela	New Year
Diwali Mela	festival of light
Hola Mohalla Mela	spring festival (in the Punjab)
the Gurpurbs	anniversaries associated with the ten Gurus

OTHER CALENDARS

CHINESE

Although the Gregorian calendar is used in China for business and official purposes, the ancient luni-solar calendar still plays an important part in everyday life. The luni-solar calendar has a cycle of 60 years. The new year begins at the first New Moon after the Sun enters the sign of Aquarius, ie between 21 January and 19 February in the Gregorian calendar.

Each year in the Chinese calendar is associated with one of 12 animals: the rat, the ox, the tiger, the rabbit, the dragon, the snake, the horse, the goat or sheep, the monkey, the chicken or rooster, the dog and the pig.

ANIMAL	YEAR								
Rat	1912	1924	1936	1948	1960	1972	1984	1996	2008
Ox	1913	1925	1937	1949	1961	1973	1985	1997	2009
Tiger	1914	1926	1938	1950	1962	1974	1986	1998	2010
Rabbit	1915	1927	1939	1951	1963	1975	1987	1999	2011
Dragon	1916	1928	1940	1952	1964	1976	1988	2000	2012
Snake	1917	1929	1941	1953	1965	1977	1989	2001	2013
Horse	1918	1930	1942	1954	1966	1978	1990	2002	2014
Goat	1919	1931	1943	1955	1967	1979	1991	2003	2015
Monkey	1920	1932	1944	1956	1968	1980	1992	2004	2016
Rooster	1921	1933	1945	1957	1969	1981	1993	2005	2017
Dog	1922	1934	1946	1958	1970	1982	1994	2006	2018
Pig	1923	1935	1947	1959	1971	1983	1995	2007	2019

CHINESE DYNASTIES
AND PERIODS
During the imperial period, the
numeration of years was based on a
complicated system of reign-titles and
other important events. The main periods
and dynasties in Chinese history are:

DATE	PERIOD/DYNASTY
	Pre-Imperial China
c.21st–16th century BC	Xia
c.16th–11th century BC	Shang
c.11th century–770 BC	Western Zhou
770–221 BC	Eastern Zhou (Spring and Autumn and Warring States periods)
	Early Empire
221–207 BC	Qin
206 BC–AD 24	Western Han
25–220	Eastern Han
220–65	Three Kingdoms (Wei, Shu and Wu)
265–316	Western Jin
	Middle Empire
317–420	Eastern Jin
420–589	Southern and Northern Dynasties
581–618	Sui
618–907	Tang
907–60	Five Dynasties
960–1127	Northern Song
1127–1279	Southern Song
	Late Empire
1279–1368	Yuan
1368–1644	Ming
1644–1911	Qing
	Post-Imperial China
1912–49	Republic
1949–present	People's Republic

JAPANESE

The Japanese calendar is essentially the same as the Gregorian calendar, the years, months and days being of the same length and beginning on the same days. The numeration of years is different, based on a system of reign-titles, each of which begins at the accession of a new emperor or other important event. The three latest epochs are defined by the reigns of emperors, whose actual names are not necessarily used:

REIGN-TITLE	DURATION
Taisho	1 August 1912 to 25 December 1926
Showa	26 December 1926 to 7 January 1989
Heisei	8 January 1989 to present

Each year of the epoch begins on 1 January and ends on 31 December.

The months are known as First Month, Second Month, etc, First Month being equivalent to January. The days of the week are:

Nichiyōbi	Sun-day
Getsuyōbi	Moon-day
Kayōbi	Fire-day
Suiyōbi	Water-day
Mokuyōbi	Wood-day
Kinyōbi	Metal-day
Doyōbi	Earth-day

ROMAN

In 46 BC Julius Caesar found that the calendar had fallen into some confusion. He sought the help of the Egyptian astronomer Sosigenes, which led to the construction and adoption in 45 BC of the Julian calendar.

In the Roman (Julian) calendar, the days of the month were counted backwards from three fixed points, or days: the Kalends, the Nones and the Ides. The Kalends was the first day of each month; the Nones fell on the fifth or seventh day; and the Ides on the 13th or 15th day, depending on the month. For example, the Ides of March was on the 15th day of the month and the days preceding the 15th were known as the seventh day before the Ides, the sixth day before the Ides, the fifth day before the Ides, etc.

The Julian calendar included an extra day in every fourth year. A year containing 366 days was called bissextilis annus because it had a doubled sixth day (bissextus dies) before the Kalends of March, ie on 24 February.

FRENCH REVOLUTIONARY

The French Revolutionary or Republican calendar was introduced in 1793. It took as its starting point 22 September 1792, the foundation of the first Republic. It was abolished in 1806 on Napoleon's orders.

The year was divided into 12 months, each of 30 days, with five or six extra days at the end. The beginning of the year was the autumnal equinox and the names of the months were intended to reflect the changes of the seasons and the activities of the agricultural year.

Vendémiaire (month of grape harvest)	23 September–22 October
Brumaire (month of mist)	23 October–21 November
Frimaire (month of frost)	22 November–21 December
Nivôse (month of snow)	22 December–20 January
Pluviôse (month of rain)	21 January–19 February
Ventôse (month of wind)	20 February–21 March
Germinal (month of buds)	22 March–20 April
Floréal (month of flowers)	21 April–20 May
Prairial (month of meadows)	21 May–19 June
Messidor (month of harvest)	20 June–19 July
Thermidor (month of heat)	20 July–18 August
Fructidor (month of fruit)	19 August–22 September

WATCHES AT SEA

First watch	8pm – midnight	Afternoon watch	midday – 4pm
Middle watch	Midnight – 4am	First dog watch	4pm – 6pm
Morning watch	4am – 8am	Last dog watch	6pm – 8pm
Forenoon watch	8am – midday		

WEDDING ANNIVERSARIES

1st	Paper	9th	Copper, or Pottery
2nd	Cotton	10th	Tin
3rd	Leather	11th	Steel
4th	Fruit and Flowers	12th	Silk and Fine Linen
5th	Wood	13th	Lace
6th	Sugar, or Iron	14th	Ivory
7th	Wool	15th	Crystal
8th	Bronze	20th	China

25th	Silver	50th	Gold
30th	Pearl	55th	Emerald
35th	Coral	60th	Diamond
40th	Ruby	70th	Platinum
45th	Sapphire		

SIGNS OF THE ZODIAC

In astronomy, the zodiac is an imaginary belt in the heavens within which lie the apparent paths of the Sun, Moon and major planets. It is bounded by two parallels generally taken as lying 8° on either side of the ecliptic or path of the Sun in its annual course. The zodiac is divided into 12 equal areas, each of 30°.

In astrology, the 12 signs of the zodiac take their names from certain of the constellations with which they once coincided; due to precession, the signs no longer coincide with the constellations whose names they bear, but astrology uses the original dates. The dates can vary slightly from year to year according to the day and hour of the Sun's transition from one sign to another; the dates given below are approximate. The signs are considered to begin at the vernal equinox with Aries.

SIGN	SYMBOL	DATES
Aries	Ram	21 March–19 April
Taurus	Bull	20 April–20 May
Gemini	Twins	21 May–21 June
Cancer	Crab	22 June–22 July
Leo	Lion	23 July–22 August
Virgo	Virgin	23 August–22 September
Libra	Balance	23 September–23 October
Scorpio	Scorpion	24 October–21 November
Sagittarius	Archer	22 November–21 December
Capricorn	Goat	22 December–19 January
Aquarius	Water Carrier	20 January–18 February
Pisces	Fishes	19 February–20 March

A 13th sign is used by some astrologers: Ophiuchus, the Serpent Bearer, the second half of Scorpio.

WEIGHTS AND MEASURES

METRIC UNITS

The metric primary standards are the metre as the unit of measurement of length, and the kilogram as the unit of measurement of mass. Other units of measurement are defined by reference to the primary standards.

MEASUREMENT OF LENGTH

Kilometre (km)	= 1,000 metres

Metre (m) is the length of the path travelled by light in a vacuum during a time interval of $\frac{1}{299792458}$ of a second

Decimetre (dm)	= $\frac{1}{10}$ metre
Centimetre (cm)	= $\frac{1}{100}$ metre
Millimetre (mm)	= $\frac{1}{1000}$ metre

MEASUREMENT OF AREA

Hectare (ha)	= 100 ares
Decare	= 10 ares
Are (a)	= 100 square metres
Square metre	= a superficial area equal to that of a square each side of which measures one metre
Square decimetre	= $\frac{1}{100}$ square metre
Square centimetre	= $\frac{1}{100}$ square decimetre
Square millimetre	= $\frac{1}{100}$ square centimetre

MEASUREMENT OF VOLUME

Cubic metre (m³)	= a volume equal to that of a cube each edge of which measures one metre
Cubic decimetre	= $\frac{1}{1000}$ cubic metre
Cubic centimetre (cc)	= $\frac{1}{1000}$ cubic decimetre
Hectolitre	= 100 litres
Litre	= a cubic decimetre
Decilitre	= $\frac{1}{10}$ litre
Centilitre	= $\frac{1}{100}$ litre
Millilitre	= $\frac{1}{1000}$ litre

MEASUREMENT OF CAPACITY

Hectolitre (hl)	= 100 litres
Litre (l or L)	= a cubic decimetre
Decilitre (dl)	= $\frac{1}{10}$ litre
Centilitre (cl)	= $\frac{1}{100}$ litre
Millilitre (ml)	= $\frac{1}{1000}$ litre

MEASUREMENT OF MASS OR WEIGHT

Tonne (t)	= 1,000 kilograms

Kilogram (kg) is equal to the mass of the international prototype of the kilogram

Hectogram (hg)	= $\frac{1}{10}$ kilogram
Gram (g)	= $\frac{1}{1000}$ kilogram
Carat, metric*	= $\frac{1}{5}$ gram
Milligram (mg)	= $\frac{1}{1000}$ gram

* Used only for transactions in precious stones or pearls

IMPERIAL UNITS

The imperial primary standards are the yard as the unit of measurement of length and the pound as the unit of measurement of mass. Other units of measurement are defined by reference to the primary standards. Most of these units are no longer authorised for use in trade in the UK.

MEASUREMENT OF LENGTH

Mile	= 1,760 yards
Furlong	= 220 yards
Chain	= 22 yards
Yard (yd)	= 0.9144 metre
Foot (ft)	= $\frac{1}{3}$ yard
Inch (in)	= $\frac{1}{36}$ yard

MEASUREMENT OF AREA

Square mile	= 640 acres
Acre	= 4,840 square yards
Rood	= 1,210 square yards
Square yard (sq. yd)	= a superficial area equal to that of a square each side of which measures one yard
Square foot (sq. ft)	= $\frac{1}{9}$ square yard
Square inch (sq. in)	= $\frac{1}{144}$ square foot

MEASUREMENT OF VOLUME

Cubic yard	= a volume equal to that of a cube each edge of which measures one yard
Cubic foot	= $\frac{1}{27}$ cubic yard
Cubic inch	= $\frac{1}{1728}$ cubic foot

MEASUREMENT OF CAPACITY

Bushel	= 8 gallons
Peck	= 2 gallons
Gallon (gal)	= 4.54609 cubic decimetres
Quart (qt)	= $\frac{1}{4}$ gallon
Pint (pt)*	= $\frac{1}{2}$ quart
Gill	= $\frac{1}{4}$ pint
Fluid ounce (fl oz)*	= $\frac{1}{20}$ pint
Fluid drachm	= $\frac{1}{8}$ fluid ounce
Minim (min)	= $\frac{1}{60}$ fluid drachm

MEASUREMENT OF MASS OR WEIGHT

Ton	= 2,240 pounds
Hundredweight (cwt)	= 112 pounds
Cental	= 100 pounds
Quarter	= 28 pounds
Stone	= 14 pounds
Pound (lb)	= 0.45359237 kilogram
Ounce (oz)	= $\frac{1}{16}$ pound
Ounce troy (oz tr)*†	= $\frac{12}{175}$ pound
Dram (dr)	= $\frac{1}{16}$ ounce
Grain (gr)	= $\frac{1}{7000}$ pound
Pennyweight (dwt)	= 24 grains
Ounce apothecaries	= 480 grains

† Used only for transactions in gold, silver or other precious metals, and articles made therefrom

METRICATION IN THE UK

From 30 September 1995, imperial units were replaced by metric units for trade and were no longer authorised for use in the UK with the exception of specialised fields listed below. Since 2007 imperial measurements can be displayed as 'supplementary indications'.

UNIT	FIELD OF APPLICATION
inch	
foot	Road traffic signs
yard	Distance and speed measurement
mile	
pint	Dispense of draught beer or cider
	Milk in returnable containers
acre	Land registration
troy ounce	Transactions in precious metals

MILLIONS AND BILLIONS

VALUE IN THE UK

Million	thousand x thousand	10^6
Billion*	million x million	10^{12}
Trillion	million x billion	10^{18}
Quadrillion	million x trillion	10^{24}

VALUE IN THE USA

Million	thousand x thousand	10^6
Billion*	thousand x million	10^9
Trillion	million x million	10^{12}
Quadrillion	million x billion US	10^{15}

* The US usage of billion (i.e. 10^9) is increasingly common, and is now universally used by statisticians

PAPER SIZES

A SERIES (magazines, books)

	MM		
A0	841	x	1,189
A1	594	x	841
A2	420	x	594
A3	297	x	420
A4	210	x	297
A5	148	x	210
A6	105	x	148
A7	74	x	105
A8	52	x	74
A9	37	x	52
A10	26	x	37

BOOK SIZES

TRADITIONAL

	MM
Royal Quarto	250 × 320
Demy Quarto	220 × 290
Crown Quarto	190 × 250
Royal Octavo	150 × 250
Demy Octavo	143 × 222
Large Crown Octavo	129 × 198

MODERN

	MM
Crown Royal	210 × 280
Royal	191 × 235
Demy	152 × 229
C format paperback	143 × 222
B format or trade paperback	129 × 198
A format	111 × 175

NAUTICAL MEASURES

DISTANCE
Distance at sea is measured in nautical miles. The British standard nautical mile was 6,080 feet, but this measure has been obsolete since 1970, when the international nautical mile of 1852 metres was adopted by the Ministry of Defence.

The cable (600 feet or 100 fathoms) was a measure approximately one-tenth of a nautical mile. Such distances are now expressed in decimal parts of a sea mile or in metres.

Soundings at sea were recorded in fathoms (6 feet); depths are now expressed in metres on Admiralty charts.

SPEED
Speed is measured in nautical miles per hour, called knots. A ship moving at the rate of 30 nautical miles per hour is said to be doing 30 knots.

KNOTS	M.P.H.
1	1.1515
2	2.3030
3	3.4545
4	4.6060
5	5.7575
6	6.9090
7	8.0606
8	9.2121
9	10.3636
10	11.5151
15	17.2727
20	23.0303
25	28.7878
30	34.5454
35	40.3030
40	46.0606

DISTANCE OF THE HORIZON

The distance to the horizon can be calculated, in metric units, using the equation $D = 3.83733\sqrt{H}$ where D is the distance in kilometres and H is the height of the observer in metres, and in imperial units using the equation $D = 1.31573\sqrt{H}$ where D is the distance in miles and H is the height of the observer in feet. The resulting distances are those following a straight line from the observer to the horizon; it is not the distance along the curvature of the Earth. The difference between these two figures, however, is minimal for heights below 100km (62 miles).

HEIGHT IN METRES (FEET)	RANGE IN KM (MILES)
*1.7 (5.6)	5.0 (3.1)
5 (16)	8.6 (5.3)
10 (32.8)	12.1 (7.5)
50 (164)	27.1 (16.8)
100 (328)	38.4 (23.8)
†509 (1,670)	86.6 (53.8)
1,000 (3,281)	121.34 (75.4)
5,000 (16,404)	271.3 (168.5)
‡8,850 (29,035)	361.0 (224.2)
§9,144 (30,000)	366.9 (228.0)

* Average human height in the UK
† Height of the tallest inhabited building
(Taipei 101)
‡ Height of Mt Everest
§ Height of cruising aeroplane

WATER AND LIQUOR MEASURES

1 litre weighs 1 kg
1 cubic metre weighs 1 tonne
1 gallon weighs 10 lb

WATER FOR SHIPS
Kilderkin	= 18 gallons
Barrel	= 36 gallons
Puncheon	= 72 gallons
Butt	= 110 gallons
Tun	= 210 gallons

BOTTLES OF WINE
Traditional equivalents in standard champagne bottles:
Magnum	= 2 bottles
Jeroboam	= 4 bottles
Rehoboam	= 6 bottles
Methuselah	= 8 bottles
Salmanazar	= 12 bottles
Balthazar	= 16 bottles
Nebuchadnezzar	= 20 bottles

A quarter of a bottle is known as a nip
An eighth of a bottle is known as a baby

TEMPERATURE SCALES

The Fahrenheit scale is related to the
Celsius scale by the equations:

temperature °F = (temperature °C x 1.8)
+ 32

temperature °C = (temperature °F − 32)
÷ 1.8

°C	°F
100	212
95	203
90	194
85	185
80	176
75	167
70	158
65	149
60	140
55	131
50	122
45	113
40	104
35	95
30	86
25	77
20	68
15	59
10	50
5	41
zero	32
−5	23
−10	14
−15	5

The freezing point of water is 0°C and
32°F

The boiling point of water is 99.974°C
and 211.953°F

Body temperature varies between 36.5°C
and 37.2°C (97.70–98.9°F)

OVEN TEMPERATURES

GAS MARK	ELECTRIC °C	°F
—	110	225
—	130	250
1	140	275
2	150	300
3	170	325
4	180	350
5	190	375
6	200	400
7	220	425
8	230	450
9	240	475

CONVERSION TABLES

Bold figures equal units of either of
the columns beside them; thus: 1 cm =
0.394 inches and 1 inch = 2.540 cm

LENGTH

CENTIMETRES		INCHES
2.540	**1**	0.394
5.080	**2**	0.787
7.620	**3**	1.181
10.160	**4**	1.575
12.700	**5**	1.969
15.240	**6**	2.362
17.780	**7**	2.756
20.320	**8**	3.150
22.860	**9**	3.543
25.400	**10**	3.937
50.800	**20**	7.874
76.200	**30**	11.811
101.600	**40**	15.748
127.000	**50**	19.685
152.400	**60**	23.622
177.800	**70**	27.559

CENTIMETRES		INCHES
203.200	**80**	31.496
228.600	**90**	35.433
254.000	**100**	39.370

METRES		YARDS
0.914	**1**	1.094
1.829	**2**	2.187
2.743	**3**	3.281
3.658	**4**	4.374
4.572	**5**	5.468
5.486	**6**	6.562
6.401	**7**	7.655
7.315	**8**	8.749
8.230	**9**	9.843
9.144	**10**	10.936
18.288	**20**	21.872
27.432	**30**	32.808
36.576	**40**	43.745
45.720	**50**	54.681
54.864	**60**	65.617
64.008	**70**	76.553
73.152	**80**	87.489
82.296	**90**	98.425
91.440	**100**	109.361

KILOMETRES		MILES
1.609	**1**	0.621
3.219	**2**	1.243
4.828	**3**	1.864
6.437	**4**	2.485
8.047	**5**	3.107
9.656	**6**	3.728
11.265	**7**	4.350
12.875	**8**	4.971
14.484	**9**	5.592
16.093	**10**	6.214
32.187	**20**	12.427
48.280	**30**	18.641
64.374	**40**	24.855
80.467	**50**	31.069

KILOMETRES		MILES
96.561	**60**	37.282
112.654	**70**	43.496
128.748	**80**	49.710
144.841	**90**	55.923
160.934	**100**	62.137

AREA

SQUARE CM		SQUARE IN
6.452	**1**	0.155
12.903	**2**	0.310
19.355	**3**	0.465
25.806	**4**	0.620
32.258	**5**	0.775
38.710	**6**	0.930
45.161	**7**	1.085
51.613	**8**	1.240
58.064	**9**	1.395
64.516	**10**	1.550
129.032	**20**	3.100
193.548	**30**	4.650
258.064	**40**	6.200
322.580	**50**	7.750
387.096	**60**	9.300
451.612	**70**	10.850
516.128	**80**	12.400
580.644	**90**	13.950
645.160	**100**	15.500

SQUARE M		SQUARE YD
0.836	**1**	1.196
1.672	**2**	2.392
2.508	**3**	3.588
3.345	**4**	4.784
4.181	**5**	5.980
5.017	**6**	7.176
5.853	**7**	8.372
6.689	**8**	9.568
7.525	**9**	10.764
8.361	**10**	11.960
16.723	**20**	23.920

SQUARE M		SQUARE YD
25.084	30	35.880
33.445	40	47.840
41.806	50	59.799
50.168	60	71.759
58.529	70	83.719
66.890	80	95.679
75.251	90	107.639
83.613	100	119.599

HECTARES		ACRES
0.405	1	2.471
0.809	2	4.942
1.214	3	7.413
1.619	4	9.844
2.023	5	12.355
2.428	6	14.826
2.833	7	17.297
3.327	8	19.769
3.642	9	22.240
4.047	10	24.711
8.094	20	49.421
12.140	30	74.132
16.187	40	98.842
20.234	50	123.555
24.281	60	148.263
28.328	70	172.974
32.375	80	197.684
36.422	90	222.395
40.469	100	247.105

VOLUME

CUBIC CM		CUBIC IN
16.387	1	0.061
32.774	2	0.122
49.161	3	0.183
65.548	4	0.244
81.936	5	0.305
98.323	6	0.366
114.710	7	0.427
131.097	8	0.488

CUBIC CM		CUBIC IN
147.484	9	0.549
163.871	10	0.610
327.742	20	1.220
491.613	30	1.831
655.484	40	2.441
819.355	50	3.051
983.226	60	3.661
1147.097	70	4.272
1310.968	80	4.882
1474.839	90	5.492
1638.710	100	6.102

CUBIC M		CUBIC YD
0.765	1	1.308
1.529	2	2.616
2.294	3	3.924
3.058	4	5.232
3.823	5	6.540
4.587	6	7.848
5.352	7	9.156
6.116	8	10.464
6.881	9	11.772
7.646	10	13.080
15.291	20	26.159
22.937	30	39.239
30.582	40	52.318
38.228	50	65.398
45.873	60	78.477
53.519	70	91.557
61.164	80	104.636
68.810	90	117.716
76.455	100	130.795

LITRES		GALLONS
4.546	1	0.220
9.092	2	0.440
13.638	3	0.660
18.184	4	0.880
22.730	5	1.100
27.276	6	1.320

LITRES		GALLONS		METRIC TONNES		TONS (UK)
31.822	7	1.540		4.064	4	3.937
36.368	8	1.760		5.080	5	4.921
40.914	9	1.980		6.096	6	5.905
45.460	10	2.200		7.112	7	6.889
90.919	20	4.400		8.128	8	7.874
136.379	30	6.599		9.144	9	8.858
181.839	40	8.799		10.161	10	9.842
227.298	50	10.999		20.321	20	19.684
272.758	60	13.199		30.481	30	29.526
318.217	70	15.398		40.642	40	39.368
363.677	80	17.598		50.802	50	49.210
409.137	90	19.798		60.963	60	59.052
454.596	100	21.998		71.123	70	68.894
				81.284	80	78.737

WEIGHT (MASS)

KILOGRAMS		POUNDS		METRIC TONNES		
				91.444	90	88.579
0.454	1	2.205		101.605	100	98.421
0.907	2	4.409				
1.361	3	6.614		METRIC TONNES		TONS (US)
1.814	4	8.819		0.907	1	1.102
2.268	5	11.023		1.814	2	2.205
2.722	6	13.228		2.722	3	3.305
3.175	7	15.432		3.629	4	4.409
3.629	8	17.637		4.536	5	5.521
4.082	9	19.842		5.443	6	6.614
4.536	10	22.046		6.350	7	7.716
9.072	20	44.092		7.257	8	8.818
13.608	30	66.139		8.165	9	9.921
18.144	40	88.185		9.072	10	11.023
22.680	50	110.231		18.144	20	22.046
27.216	60	132.277		27.216	30	33.069
31.752	70	154.324		36.287	40	44.092
36.287	80	176.370		45.359	50	55.116
40.823	90	198.416		54.431	60	66.139
45.359	100	220.464		63.503	70	77.162
				72.575	80	88.185
				81.647	90	99.208
METRIC TONNES		TONS (UK)		90.719	100	110.231
1.016	1	0.984				
2.032	2	1.968				
3.048	3	2.953				

CLOTHING SIZE CONVERSIONS

MEN'S

ITEM	UK	USA	EUROPE
Suits	36	36	46
	38	38	48
	40	40	50
	42	42	52
	44	44	54
	46	46	56
Shirts	14	14	36
	14½	14½	37
	15	15	38
	15½	15½	39–40
	16	16	41
	16½	16½	42
	17	17	43
	17½	17½	44–45
Shoes	6½	7	39
	7	7½	40
	7½	8	41
	8	8½	42
	8½	9	43
	9	9½	43
	9½	10	44
	10	10½	44
	10½	11	45

WOMEN'S

ITEM	UK	USA	EUROPE
Clothing	8	6	36
	10	8	38
	12	10	40
	14	12	42
	16	14	44
	18	16	46
	20	18	48
	22	20	50
	24	22	52
Shoes	4	5½	37
	4½	6	37
	5	6½	38
	5½	7	38
	6	7½	39
	6½	8	39
	7	8½	40
	7½	9	40
	8	9½	41